SHORT STORY WRITING

THE WRITERS NEWS LIBRARY OF WRITING

SHORT STORY WRITING

Dilys Gater

DStJT
WN

British Library Cataloguing in Publication Data
Gater, Dilys
  Short Story Writing. – ("Writers News"
  Library of Writing; Vol. 5)
  I. Title II. Series
  808.3

  ISBN 0 946537 83 6 (Hardback)
       0 946537 85 2 (Paperback)

Printed in Great Britain by BPCC Wheatons Ltd, Exeter
for David St John Thomas Publisher,
PO Box 4, Nairn, Scotland IV12 4HU

CONTENTS

PART V THE COMMERCIAL PRODUCT

PART VI A STORYTELLER'S LIFE

INTRODUCTION

There cannot be many writers who have not tried their hand at short story writing at some time or other. Short story writing may not be their particular field – they may be novelists, article writers or whatever – but few of them will have been able to resist the appeal of the short story. The reason is of course that short story writing is creatively challenging and satisfying at the same time.

In the space of just a few thousand words, the story has to create a fictional world, to introduce characters with whom the readers come to identify, show how those characters deal with a given set of circumstances, and to reach a conclusion that the reader feels is exactly right. To achieve all these things within a limited word count is nothing less than an art form.

Its wide appeal as an art form is evident from the hundreds of stories that arrive at *Writers News* as entries in our monthly short story writing competitions. It is also evident from the vast number of stories that arrive on the desks of the fiction editors at the various women's magazines; as one of them put it to me recently: 'The whole world must be writing short stories.'

The same editor went on to explain that screening all these stories – reading through them to select the ones most suitable for publication – is not as difficult as you might think. And what she had to say is consistent with our own experience of judging competition entries at *Writers News*.

The fact is that the great majority of short stories that an editor (or a competition judge) gets to see can best be described as 'average'. They are written competently enough, but they are neither better nor worse than most of the other stories on the pile. Usually, as many as 90 percent of stories fall into this average category.

There is, of course, another 5 percent that fall well below average. Mostly, they are first efforts from people whose writing skills still need to be polished before they stand any chance of success. That leaves the other 5 percent: the stories that are really good, and that have genuine sparkle. These are the ones that earn their way onto the shortlist and are seriously considered for publication.

If you enjoy using words, and have some latent writing skills, it does not take very long to graduate from the 'below average' 5 percent. That is not really the problem. The problem is how to write stories that are better than average, and which take you into that top 5 percent.

The good news is that the skills you need to write good short stories happen to be skills that can be taught. Of course, all writing skills can be taught to some extent or other and can therefore be learnt. But the learning experience is of particular relevance to the short story writer. The disciplines of writing fiction within a short word count – the disciplines of the art form – depend very much on the right techniques.

The dictionary defines technique as practical method, and this is a good definition for us. It reminds us that the techniques of short story writing are practical methods, not fanciful theories about creativity and inspiration. It also reminds us that good short story writers are made not born.

Yes, of course you have to be born with a love for words and a wish to express yourself and your ideas. But you would not be interested in writing in the first place if you were not born with these qualities. These are qualities that provide your basic motivation, that make you want to write short stories. But to become a good short story writer you need more: you need to learn the practical methods.

Let us look at a small example of these practical methods at work. Let us start with your idea for a short story: imagine you have reached the point at which you know what your story is going to be about, you know what is going to happen in it. Before you rush to commit your story to paper, your first task – your first practical task – should be to write down a brief description of the storyline, a brief explanation of what happens to whom.

If you cannot write this explanation in less than twenty words, the probability is that your idea is too complex for the confines of a short story. So at once you have applied a practical test, and have demonstrated to yourself that your idea needs more thinking about before it can be expressed in short story form. There is no magic about this '20 word' test; it is just one of the practical methods, one of the techniques, that any writer can be taught to use.

That, of course, is only a basic example of what is meant by technique. It does not help you with the problems of characterisation, dialogue, pacing and so forth that you are going to tackle as a short story writer. But Dilys Gater is able to help you with problems such as these. Dilys has a great deal of experience both in writing short stories (and, as it happens, also in writing novels) and in teaching writing skills. In this book, she has brought together her very wide experience and focused it on the one big question: how do you write short stories that will make it to the top 5 percent?

Once you can write stories as well as that, a whole world is open to you. We have already mentioned the short story slots in women's magazines, but that is only part of the picture. There are many competitions open to short story writers which are enjoyable to enter, and which can help to establish a writer's name; many of them publish anthologies of the best entries, and it is always nice to see your work in print in this way. And there is a whole field of small press magazines that publish short stories; many of them do not pay much (if at all) but a good number of writers have first made their mark in this way. Perhaps even more important than writing for any of these markets is the sheer enjoyment that comes from writing short stories. As I said earlier, in creative terms it is a form of writing that is both challenging and satisfying. And if you have met a challenge to your own satisfaction, that cannot be bad.

Richard Bell
Editor, *Writers News*

AUTHOR'S NOTE

I should like to express my appreciation and indebtedness towards the authors mentioned in these pages. Without models to study and to provide inspiration no student of the art and craft of storytelling would be able to recognise excellence, let alone aim to achieve it.

Dilys Gater

PART I
BASICS

1
CLEARING THE GROUND

So you want to become a successful writer of short stories, and you would like some helpful advice as to how to go about it. Believe it or not, if you have that basic aim clear in your mind, you have already made a step along the road to achieving your ambition.

The main problem facing would-be writers of short stories is that, right at the beginning of their writing careers, they attempt short stories without being aware exactly what a short story is. This may sound so obvious it is not worth mentioning; but it remains a fact that many new writers do not even realise there is a difference between fact and fiction.

Problems like this seem to would-be writers to be rather shaming, and to spring from their own inadequacy rather than anything else, so they are hardly ever brought out into the light of day. Consequently, the new writer remains in ignorance, as well as in an ever-increasing state of frustration. People in this position can drift into producing any old sort of manuscript without first establishing their aims clearly in their minds – what they are trying to do and how they intend to set about it.

There are good reasons why prospective authors can find themselves grappling helplessly with their short stories, tangling themselves up in their writing, unable to proceed and with no real clue as to where they are going. Consider the prospects facing the beginner when he sits down at the start of his writing career with a blank sheet of paper before him. There are three rough categories of work which, by and large, cover most types of writing he might attempt.

One is non-fiction, usually in the form of articles for magazines (few new writers think of attempting a full-length non-fiction book); the second is fiction, in the form of a novel; and the third is fiction in the form of short stories. There are other forms such as writing for the stage or writing for radio or tv, but we will not concern ourselves with these at present. The first important decision a beginner must make is whether to write non-fiction or fiction.

Many new authors tend to steer clear of articles, and prefer to attempt fiction. And since it is commonly (though erroneously) believed that novels and short stories are much the same thing, except that it takes longer to write a novel and involves more work, the would-be author makes the decision to become a short story writer. He finds himself in the position we are now considering: wanting to write short stories but not really understanding what is required, or how to set about it.

The would-be short story writer is often unaware that he is not equipped to tackle such an undertaking, and once again doubts his own ability when he finds the going diffi-cult. But bear in mind that in the course of an ordinary – even a good – general education, the art, craft, technique – call it what you will – of professional writing is rarely on the curriculum. Yet it is something that needs to be learnt.

The fact that the average person has never been taught how to write articles for magazines, or the secrets of writing a novel, is glaringly obvious to all, and writers who decide to attempt articles or a novel will go out automatically to buy reference books and set about educating themselves in the techniques.

But short stories are a different matter. We all know how to tell a story, we might even have 'kept the children quiet' with tales they long to hear over and over. Or we might have a reputation among our friends and relatives as a great spinner of yarns. We might well feel that if we have a flair for spinning tales, we are well qualified to undertake the writing of short stories. Surely, writing a short story that will please an editor is not so very different to telling the kids that thunder is no more than 'the angels moving the furniture round in heaven' and elaborating on this theme whenever there is a storm.

In fact, there is all the difference in the world between making up stories in an everyday, amateurish sort of way (or even writing these stories down for the benefit of our family and the fellow members of the local writers circle) and approaching the writing of short stories in a serious and professional manner.

This form of writing often seems as though it is a first step, as though it will gently ease the new writer into what he sees as more difficult types of writing like non-fiction and novels. But in fact, the opposite is the case. A short story – a good short story – is one of the most difficult things a writer can attempt. It needs skills and techniques the amateur storyteller is hardly even aware of. But these skills can be learnt, and in this book we are going to start from scratch, putting aside any misconceptions which might have plagued us and hindered us from progressing in the past.

First, we need some sort of definition. What, exactly, is a short story? The term is double misleading, since the length of short stories can vary from under 1,000 words (these are called a 'short-short') to maybe 10,000 or even more words. Much will depend on what the story itself is about, and also the requirements of the editor the writer hopes will buy and publish it.

And the term 'story' is extremely vague. Many types of written work can be lumped together under the general heading of a story. It might even appear on first glance that they have nothing at all in common. There are short stories which have succeeded as a one-off and will never fit into any conventional set of rules; some are intensely poetic, with the poetry seeming to take wing from the story's foothold in reality; others are written to a strict formula in order to sell to a commercial market such as a women's magazine. Yet each one, in its own way, might be an excellent story.

We will be examining this situation in more detail later. At this stage, all we need to be aware of, as a working definition, is that a short story is a prose work of fiction, of variable length. A short story does not consist of a series of facts or incidents that really happened. It may be based on facts, but those facts should be selectively used to further the story, rather than for their own sake.

Some people confuse writing a story with the type of essay-writing they might have done in school. An essay does not tell a story, it expresses the author's views on any given topic. Though short anecdotes might be used to illustrate some point the author wants to make, they do not constitute a short story. A short story presents to the reader, from start to finish, a group of imaginary characters whom the author has invented. It details – in ways we will be discussing in this book – the incidents and happenings which befall them.

An imaginative account of *A Picnic at the Seaside* or even *Life in a Harem* or *The Day I saw a Ghost* does not make a short story. Get all these differences clear in your mind. They are basic and fundamental, yet they might take some time to register, and the reason they need emphasis is because, incredibly, it remains a fact that even would-be writers who have read several books on how to write short stories often end up feeling they know less about the short story than they did at the beginning.

What I am trying to achieve is a voice sitting by a fireplace telling you a story on a winter's evening.

Truman Capote

2
WRITING TO SELL – OR WRITING FOR YOURSELF?

There are two ways of approaching short stories – or indeed any other form of writing if it comes to that. But particularly short stories since, as we have seen, the scope of the short story writer appears at first glance to be the widest and least limiting in almost all its aspects.

It rather appears, the beginner might well think, that you can write a short story about practically anything, in whatever way you like, and almost anybody will publish it. Even those who pause to consider what rules they will need to keep to if they tackle an article or a novel, will happily throw all restraints aside when they set about writing a short story. Once again, the same misconceptions we have touched on earlier can be found in the attitudes of new writers towards this form of writing.

It is widely believed that a short story is not only easy to write, but very likely easy to sell. So some newcomers view them as a fast and relatively effortless way of making money. Others, more humbly, feel that this is an art form they would like to learn, and are more interested in acquiring the necessary skills, though they will not deny that they dream of publication some day 'when I'm good enough'. Even they might cherish a hope that in due course, they will begin to reap monetary rewards for their labours.

There is nothing wrong with aiming high. All writers feel a need to communicate, and most dream of seeing their work in print – hopefully, of being paid for the privilege too. But even before you put pen to paper, you need to be sure you are writing stories for the right reasons.

Be honest with yourself. Is it just the thought of all those fat cheques with a lot of noughts on them that is prompting your striving for a literary career? If it is, then the best advice I can give is that you get a part-time job as a barman or an Avon lady. You will get rich far quicker than by bombarding innocent editors, who have never done you any harm, with sheafs of unsolicited stories.

Does this mean the hopeful aspirant is never likely to sell anything, then? I can hear you asking. Indeed, no, and for those practical people who will benefit from a streamlined consumer-friendly approach to the question of marketing their wares, it is significant that many authorities now choose to deal with stories (as well as other forms of writing) as a product which needs market research and study in order to sell, rather than twittering discussions held in hushed tones about inspiration and art.

The two ways of approaching the writing of stories are therefore firstly a practical one (because you like writing stories and would like to make this a rewarding part of your life in every way if it becomes possible) and secondly a voca- tional one (which incorporates the artistic and literary side; you want to fulfil the need to explore your dreams, to create, to make some sort of statement).

The purely practical approach is much easier to deal with, and might well provide all the motivation some writers need to start them on their way to success. The vocational and inspirational side of things we will leave aside for the moment before we examine it in detail further on. It may come as rather a shock to the more dedicated writers to learn that it is entirely possible to write and sell short stories which are largely superficial and have little or no artistic value. Indeed, the editors who accept such stories would turn down anything artistic as soon as they had scanned the first page. In the same way that some of the programmes which are shown on tv and some of the films which keep appearing on the circuits can be loosely categorised as appealing to the shallowest level of intellect, and do not contain anything that remotely resembles the great – or even the good – in the form of art, so there are openings for writers of short stories who

can turn out 'formula' type stories that make easy, unde-
manding reading, contain all the right ingredients and do not
upset the readers by bringing social problems, injustices or
anything unpleasant to their attention.

Prospective writers are inclined to knock the commercial
sort of story and declare loudly that they do not want to be
associated with such pathetic rubbish. Such people take
Hemingway or some other cult figure as their literary god,
and shudder at the very thought of writing short stories for,
say, a romantic women's magazine. But though we will be
exploring all the inspirational, artistic and other aspects of
this art form, we would be wise to bear in mind that there is
room for every sort of talent in the literary marketplace. Even
though the writers of commercial formula stories may never
produce great works of genius, they have a talent for bringing
a hopeful and uplifting moment in a humdrum day to their
readers. What is more, writing a commercial formula story is
not as easy as it looks. If you doubt this, try it and see.

STUDYING A MARKET

In order to study a market and write for it, you need to treat
each story you attempt as purely a commercial product,
written for one particular slot in one particular market.
Basically, this method of working runs along the following
lines:

First decide the magazine or periodical (or other market
such as a radio programme) that you aim to contribute to.
Then soak yourself in the requirements of this market by
reading several issues of the periodical or listening to the
radio programme or whatever. Every magazine, newspaper,
journal and programme on radio or tv has its own particular
style, its own particular angle or format. You can attempt to
identify this if you work hard at your market study. As a
general rule, once you have made a clinical analysis of the
market for which you propose to write, you will be able to
produce a story that stands a far greater chance of acceptance
since it will be tailormade to suit the demands of that particular market.

As a guide to market study, you need to examine your chosen magazine or periodical over as many issues as possible: perhaps six; more if you are still unsure of what the editor is looking for. When you think you have a good idea, draw up a report to which you can refer when you come to write a story for this market. The following questions will help you to compile your report:

1. Does your chosen magazine/periodical/radio programme regularly use short stories? How many per issue?

2. What is the average number of words required per story?

3. What sort of writing style seems to be favoured? Formal or more chatty? Are paragraphs long or short? And what about the length of sentences?

4. Is there a lot of description or is the preference for terse, fast-moving narrative?

5. Is the story usually told in the first person by one of the characters speaking as *I*? Or is it in the third person, where the action is viewed through the eyes of the author as narrator?

6. What sort of people does the average story feature – dwellers in council houses or the county set? Is there a masculine or feminine viewpoint?

7. What sort of situations are favoured – family problems, romance and love, detective or crime for example?

8. How much dialogue is used? Is it mostly just a line here and there, or are there long speeches?

9. What sort of people do you think the readers are? Young, mature or elderly? What sort of homes will they live in? (You can fill in on this point by examining the other contents of your chosen periodical or magazine, especially the advertise-

ments. If there seems to be a preponderance of adverts for home lifts, toupees and herbal cures for aching joints and wrinkles, for instance, it is safe to assume that the readers are not going to be school-leavers whose most pressing concern is what to do about puppy fat and acne!)

Try to put together as comprehensive a picture as you can of the sort of story this particular magazine might be likely to take. Each magazine, periodical and paper has its own particular requirements, and the editor is unlikely to bend his policy for something that, though touching his flinty heart and reducing all his staff to tears, is not the sort of story the magazine uses.

One very important rule when you are actually attempting to sell your work (and something which many new writers refuse to acknowledge) is that even a story written by a recognised genius will be rejected if it does not conform to the requirements of that particular market. Editors and publishers are, first and foremost, businessmen, and they expect the writers who submit stories to them to be similarly businesslike in their approach. So never kid yourself that an editor will bend the rules just for you. Though it comes as a shock to some aspirants to short story success, you must always bear in mind that the literary world has been progressing very nicely thank you for many decades without you, and it is perfectly capable of doing so in the future. It is your job to persuade editors they need you; they are not there to provide you with a helping hand.

All of this should explain why many authorities on short story writing advocate this sort of clinical approach. To be successful, it appears, the writer must study closely what his chosen editor is looking for, and then aim to provide him with exactly that. By comparative analysis, rather like feeding data into a computer and waiting for a print-out to appear, the writer will then be able to put together a story which is exactly right, even down to the last sentence, the last comma and full stop.

As we have seen, this analytical approach might well appeal to a certain type of writer. But others will probably regard it as a fast-buck, Writing By Numbers attitude, and as such find it disturbing and unacceptable. If you are one of them, you may not be able to explain just why you feel this way. Indeed, in some cases, a reluctance to carry out the necessary market study of such details as length, style, content and suitability for the market smacks suspiciously of one of the mysterious ailments writers can suffer as soon as they sit down to write – it is known commonly as sheer laziness, and can be the ruination of many a promising writing career.

But no. You will be in good company if you are feeling that surely there must be more to it than just weighing up all the right ingredients and then churning out custom-made stories en masse. Indeed, there is... a great deal more.

There are three reasons for becoming a writer: the first is that you need the money; the second, that you have something to say that you think the world should know; the third is that you can't think what to do with the long winter evenings.
Quentin Crisp

3
FINDING
YOUR VOICE

Here are the opening paragraphs of two short stories for you to consider. The first:

'When Mr Hiram B. Otis, the American Minister, bought Canterville Chase, every one told him he was doing a very foolish thing, as there was no doubt at all that the place was haunted. Indeed, Lord Canterville himself, who was a man of the most punctilious honour, had felt it his duty to mention the fact to Mr Otis, when they came to discuss terms.'

The second:

'During the whole of a dull, dark and soundless day in the autumn of the year, when the clouds hung oppressively low in the heavens, I had been passing alone, on horseback, through a singularly dreary tract of country; and at length found myself, as the shades of the evening drew on, within view of the melancholy House of Usher. I know not how it was – but, with the first glimpse of the building, a sense of insufferable gloom pervaded my spirit.'

Both of these stories were written by masters of the short story form. The first example is the opening of Oscar Wilde's *The Canterville Ghost*; the second – if you have not guessed already – is from *The Fall of the House of Usher* by Edgar Allan Poe.

In both cases, the story concerns the supernatural, but here the resemblance ends. Oscar Wilde's story, detailed with a sure, though light, touch is a hilarious account of the efforts

23

of the Canterville Ghost to keep up his traditional hauntings in the face of a refusal on the part of the American family, who now occupy his ancestral home, to take him seriously. Poe's story, by contrast, is a brooding and melancholy exercise in horror.

When an author sits down to write a story – especially an inexperienced author – he often feels he must impose a literary or some other elevated style on what he writes. His own words do not seem to be enough, they seem to be rather feeble and paltry, and he may look around for an example to copy, or start expressing what he wants to say in much more flowery language than he would normally use.

So before we proceed to the actual writing of your story, we must first consider you, the writer. For contrary to the commonly-held belief that it is the story which is all-important, yawning ahead of the writer like some sort of gigantic jigsaw puzzle where the writer's task is to fit each piece in the right place to make it work, it is the writer himself who really matters.

A story is only an appendage, an extension of its writer and what he thinks and feels. With luck, his brainchild will in due course take on a life of its own, stand on its own two feet, as it were. But even so, a story still expresses something which is inherently its author, something which is unique to that author's personality.

So many new writers sit down to write a story and are frustrated to find they do not know exactly what they should include. They feel the story makes demands on them which they are unable to meet. If only I knew what to put in, they say despairingly, then the story would be fine. They are certain there is some magical list of ingredients which, shaken up together, will result in a satisfactory end product.

But consider the two examples above. Did Wilde approach his ghost story or Poe his study in melancholic horror in this manner? If they had done so, their stories might well have been far more similar in style, both on a supernatural theme as they are. They would also have been superficially alike in their effect on the reader. And if the stories themselves were already waiting, wanting only the hand of a writer to record them – any writer, whoever got there first – we can take it that Poe might have been known to us as the author of an amusing tale about the Canterville Ghost, while Oscar Wilde might have been modestly satisfied with a new opus called *The Fall of the House of Usher*.

But instead, each story can be recognised immediately as bearing the stamp of the man who wrote it. The reason why it is impossible to mistake a story by Oscar Wilde – or any other great writer – for a story by Edgar Allan Poe, is not because of the story itself, but because it was written by that one particular author.

There are no such things as great stories – or even moderately good stories – hovering round us in the ether, waiting to be plucked from the air and pinned down onto the page by somebody who is lucky enough to come across them. There are only the individual authors, each writing in their own way, producing their own individual work. You and I, as well as Wilde and Poe and all the other aspirants who at some time or another set out to write short stories, are all in the same boat. The difference between the greats and the beginners is simply that the beginners have more to learn. But nobody is born with an innate talent for being able to write perfect short stories without any study or practise. Even recognised masters who seem as though they can run off a fantastic tale at the flick of a finger, had to start somewhere. They too had to toil and slave at their work, polishing it, editing it, putting their hopes and dreams into it, in a continual striving to achieve their goal.

When you consider your own work, and are honest about how you rate yourself as a writer, you might well feel that, though you have a burning desire to create something good, you are full of doubts as to your ability to do so. But there is one important fact you are probably not aware of. Indeed, you may not believe it, but I can assure you that it is true.

Every writer (including yourself) is unique and possesses his or her own distinctive style, his or her own special voice. If you and I were to write a story each on the same subject, the stories would be completely different because one had come from your own particular view of the world, of life and living, expressed in your own particular way, and the other had come from mine. Even if we wanted to resolve our differences and write in the same way, such a thing would be impossible. So whatever you think about your writing, however you view it, you have to remember that even if at present it is shaky and faltering and does not seem to know exactly where it is heading, it is – even at this stage – something you can start to take a pride in, something special and unique to you, which is worth taking pains over.

You may not be aware of your own style, your own voice. You will probably not even be able to recognise it now that it has been brought to your attention. But it is there, and if you try to write in flowery or literary language, or in any other way which will not allow your own voice to be heard, you will be hindering your own progress. Be yourself. Write honestly, from your own mind and your own heart, and do not at this stage judge yourself too harshly. Let your own special way of expressing yourself have a chance to grow. What the beginner needs more than anything is confidence, both in his abilities and in what he is trying to achieve.

You might continue to feel awkward when you express yourself in a creative manner. But the possibilities become much more exciting when you stop thinking of writing a story as some sort of test where you have to keep coming up with all the right answers, where you are at the mercy of your own creation. Start to realise that you, the author, are in control of what you are doing. You do not have to prove anything to anyone, and you can work at your own pace, doing what you choose to do when you choose to do it.

But even though each author has his own voice, his own distinctive style, there is one fact which beginners never seem to consider: you will never be a good writer if you do not have something to say.

Obvious, you think? Not so, for this runs alongside the belief (which we have seen to be misguided) that good plots exist in some invisible dimension, and that if an author can only find the key to this stockpile of literary wonders, he will turn overnight into a rich and famous master of his trade and will never have to sweat over his typewriter again.

All the ingredients which make a story good come from within the writer, not from without. And in the same way that the author needs to be in control of his story rather than the other way about, he has to draw on his own resources for the message he wants to put across. If he has no message, nothing he wants passionately to communicate to his readers, no experience he wants to share, no wounds he wants healed, no blessings he wants to give thanks for, no wisdom that life has taught him – then he might as well give up trying to write short stories and spend the time playing croquet or ten-pin bowling.

There is no chance at all for the writer whose mind is dry and arid, and who finds nothing he feels he wants to say to his fellow man. But equally, there is no chance for the aspiring writer who fills up reams of paper saying far too much in the manner of a soapbox orator. Direct messages like 'Ban the Bomb' or 'Freedom from Famine' or 'Legalise Abortion', or any other cause which is strongly felt by the author, may be entirely praiseworthy as a cause, but should never be the sole motivation for a short story. Fiction, as we have seen earlier, is an art form. It is not a soapbox and will never work if you use it in order to persuade your readers of your own deeply-felt convictions.

So exactly what do we mean when we say that a writer needs to have something to say?

We are all apprentices in a craft where no one ever becomes a master.

Ernest Hemingway

Fiction gives counsel. It connects the present with the past, and the visible with the invisible. It distributes the suffering. It says we must compose ourselves in our stories in order to exist. It says if we don't do it, someone else will do it for us.

E.L. Doctorow

Why shouldn't truth be stranger than fiction? Fiction, after all, has to make sense.

Mark Twain

4
STOP, LOOK, LISTEN!

While there might seem to be very great differences between the classic short stories written a century or so ago, and the sort of stories the writer of today should be trying to produce, the methods remain largely the same. And so, advice which applied to short story writing in the past is often just as valid today.

Guy de Maupassant was arguably the greatest writer of short stories in France, if not in the world. He owed a great deal to his friend and tutor, the novelist Gustave Flaubert, who, on deciding the young Maupassant showed promise at writing prose, spent years tutoring him in the art of writing. But we are told that before he progressed to writing, Maupassant first had to satisfy his mentor that he was proficient in what we can refer to as the use of the 'Writer's Eye' – the art of seeing.

'There is a part of everything which is unexplored,' said Flaubert, 'because we are accustomed to using our eyes only in association with the memory of what people before us have thought of the thing we are looking at. Even the smallest thing has something in it which is unknown. We must find it.'

The writer Anaïs Nin explains this process another way:

'It is the function of art to renew our perception. What we are familiar with we cease to see. The writer shakes up the familiar scene, and as if by magic we see a new meaning in it.'

As an aspiring writer of short stories, you need to be aware that it is this art of seeing, the way you 'shake up the familiar scene', which will provide you with things to say, things to reveal, examine and comment on in your work. As we have heard, the writer is obliged to draw on his own resources in order to create, and it is highly unlikely that a person who takes no notice of the everyday things that go on around him, the behaviour of other people, the events and incidents that happen from moment to moment, will ever write a successful piece of fiction.

The raw material of the writer is life and the people who live it, and it is by making a conscious effort to STOP! LOOK! and LISTEN! to all the teeming details of life around you that you will begin to acquire the Writer's Eye which will bring conviction, reality and truth to what you write and assist you to write well.

You may feel you already take notice of what goes on around you, you are already aware of the things that happen. Surely you have more than enough of a Writer's Eye to be able to write a good story? Only you can decide on this, but remember that a good writer never reaches a point where he does not have to take notice. He does it instinctively, because it has become something he takes as much for granted as cleaning his teeth. To a genuine, committed writer, looking and listening is more than just an exercise, it is his whole way of life.

But how can you be sure you are looking at the right things, you may wonder. Nothing very noteworthy may be happening around you – but it is this same ordinary, everyday trivia which you, with your Writer's Eye will illumine for your readers, so that they in their turn see new meanings. Stop for a moment here and now. Are you aware of the sounds you can hear? Take a pen and paper, randomly, without any preparation, and list everything you can hear.

While you list them, jot down any meanings you attach to these sounds, emotions they arouse in you, or facts they bring home to you.

As an example list, I did the same exercise. Here is what I wrote in reply to the question 'What Can I Hear?':

'The soft click of my word processor as I work (hope to goodness my ribbon is not going to run out)

'The distant roar of a plane passing overhead (going to land at Heathrow, they pass over this part of London about every thirty seconds. As I watch them, the lights twinkling in the night sky, or silver against a blue sky, like some giant bird, I think of the awesome responsibility of the air traffic controllers, with all these planes held in a descending spiral, each one only thirty seconds from a potential disaster if they should fail even by a hairs-breadth to keep to the instructions they are given –)

'The slight, soft creak of my clothes, as I move in my chair. How can I describe the movement of my leather top – it must be something like the buckskin worn in the old West – a soft shirring sound. I wonder if people realise that it is practically impossible to move quietly when you are wearing leather? Even my jeans make a soft sound as I ease my feet, and the motion travels up my leg muscles, from my ankles to my calves.

'Just one car passing outside, but I can hear another, more powerful some distance away. A car horn somewhere – and now the overlapping of several car engines. It seems odd when I can hear nothing, when the traffic is quiet.

'Almost ghostlike, the breeze tossing the branches of the tree in the courtyard outside my window. The white blossom is already fading, the cobbles are covered with white petals already turning brown. The branches whisper, just barely whisper. And where are the birds this morning? Normally the pigeons are making sounds that remind me of the cooing of doves – .'

In addition to making a list for yourself of what you can hear, try another where you list what you can see. And then of what you can feel. The everyday things with which you are so familiar will assume new forms when you view them through a writer's eye. How would the mundane, humdrum sounds and sights of your daily routine seem to a stranger – a reader who might be perusing your list?

In what you write, you will allow your readers to view the realities of life and living through *your* eyes. Because you are an individual and you look at life in your own way, they might well find that some aspect of living which had seemed ordinary to them before – boring, even – is suddenly illuminated by the things you tell them, the incidents you detail to them.

'If only I had thought of that myself,' they might say. 'If only I had realised that side of things. But I have never looked at it from that angle before. It explains a lot. I am so glad I read this story.'

In my own comparatively short exploration of the sounds I was aware of, there were several thoughts that might, if I felt I needed inspiration, have given me the germ of a short story. We will be dealing with this subject further on, but my example does illustrate that, contrary to what many new writers believe, ideas and subject matter for stories need not be glamorous and exotic. In fact, the experiences of those who lead glamorous and exotic lives are far beyond the reach of ordinary mortals.

One of the most vital pieces of advice any new writer can receive is to write about what you know. Indeed, you may well have already come across this idea, and thought privately to yourself that the person who said it quite obviously had no idea at all of what it was like to be just an ordinary, everyday person, living an ordinary, everyday life. If he or she *had* known what it was like to be ordinary, you may well have thought, they would have realised that there was absolutely nothing to interest any reader in the events of your own routine existence.

But the advice to write about what you know does not mean you should confine yourself to the boundaries of your own daily existence, and if you are a housewife (for example) never attempt to write about any character other than a housewife exactly like yourself. If you happen to be a plumber, you need not feel you are only qualified to write stories involving plumbers.

When I was twelve years old, I can remember entering a Short Story Competition in a national newspaper. If I had kept to what I knew, even at that tender age, I might have produced a reasonably good story centred on my own daily existence as a schoolgirl with great dreams, wonderful aspirations of becoming a famous author. The whole story could have been of the rainbows that lit up my life, the bitterness of the rejections, the feelings of my own unworthiness and inability – all of this would have made my story special to me and my own particular kind of knowledge. But it never occurred to me that a story could be written about such an ordinary, plain person (in my eyes) as myself, and the story I wrote for the competition was called *Trapeze Act* and was set in a circus – of which, needless to say, I had no first-hand experience at all. As a result, I was a runner-up – but if I had used my own thoughts and feelings rather than trying to imagine what it felt like to lose your nerve if you were a trapeze artist in a circus, I might have been the winner.

This classic error of judgement has raised its ugly head and leered at me on many occasions since then. Do not let the same thing happen to you. There was no one to instruct me about keeping to what I knew – but you can benefit from my mistake.

When you begin to look around you with a Writer's Eye you will find that even the cobwebs and grease of dirty housework, the annoyance of the way 'that woman next door' corners you and keeps you talking over the fence for almost an hour, not to mention the lovely things like birthdays, Christmas, spring flowers, sunlight and the silky feel of your cat's fur – all these and so many more will take on qualities you would never have suspected. And the more you use your seeing abilities, the wider your scope will become. It is not necessary to write only about what you know, but you need the foundation of your own personal experience to assist you as you begin to roam further afield. And keeping to familiar pathways when you are beginning your writing career will give you confidence.

The things that make a short story real, authentic, are the woven threads we all experience in our lives – love, pain, joy, grief, passion, boredom, fear, rage, hate. Once you have begun to be aware of what is taking place around you, once you have begun to use your Writer's Eye, once you have started to train yourself to watch and observe, not just to take life for granted, you will find the things you want to put into your writing, the things you want to say.

This is one of the most exciting moments a writer can experience, the sudden realisation that he wants to share so many things with his reader that he can hardly wait to get them onto the page. Writing is meant to be like this, thrilling, uplifting, exhilarating. It does not always work out this way, but these moments of urgency and communication do make up for the hard parts, when the going is tough and the writer is tempted to drop the whole thing and forget it.

You will find, once you actively start cultivating your Writer's Eye, that everything around you becomes fascinating, rather than mundane. And you will feel that in a way, you are an adventurer, an explorer, treading new paths and making discoveries that will thrill your readers.

As an example of how very different your life is going to be, consider the following comment on the nature of a writer: he is the person who goes to a strip-tease show in order to watch the audience.

There is only one trait that marks the writer. He is always watching. It's a kind of trick of mind and he is born with it.
Morley Callaghan

What no wife of a writer can ever understand is that a writer is working when he's staring out the window.
Burton Rascoe

PART II
THE SHORT STORY

5
WHAT IS A SHORT STORY?

A short story is many things. But first and foremost it is just that: a story with a beginning, a middle and an end. You cannot have a story where nothing happens, just as you cannot have a story with no characters in it. A story tells of what happened to the characters who are involved, over a chronological period of time.

A story has to do more than just detail incidents, however. The incidents have to be fitted together so that certain rules of storytelling are fulfilled. A story has to tell the reader much more than just what happened next.

Every good short story (and even those which are not so good) should have some sort of message that can be summed up in one sentence. What does a story in a popular woman's magazine tell its readers? In most cases that 'love conquers all' or 'love will find a way'. The simpler the story, the easier it is to pick out the message, though the same message might be the inspiration for a much more subtle, complex work.

You do not have to rack your brains to think of complicated, original themes for your stories. The message needs to be kept relatively simple or it will become lost in the complicated machinations of the plot. And even the great masters of the short story have used a relatively small selection of themes over the years. You might wish to tell the readers of your crime stories that 'crime will not pay' or 'the criminal punishes himself more severely than any outside force can do'. You might find inspiration in themes such as 'the most frightening thing is fear itself', 'by facing up to our fears, we overcome them' or 'by setting those we love free to leave us, we ensure their return'.

It is not the theme or message itself which is the most

important thing – almost any truism, proverb or epigram you can think of will certainly have been used many times before by someone else. What matters is the way you present it. In other words, it is not what you say that makes a story good, it is the way you say it.

But you will help yourself a great deal if you start compiling a list of interesting themes and messages which might at some future date inspire you with the germ of an idea for a story. Often, if you find (as you are certain to do at some stage or another in your writing career) that you are not in the right frame of mind to write, you can browse through notes you might like to keep for this very purpose. A great deal of a writer's work is done on a subconscious level, and the most unlikely ideas might suddenly and very unexpectedly take root in your mind when you least expect it.

Here are a few interesting topics to start you off:

Complete honesty between husband and wife will probably lead to disaster.

We do not value the things we obtain easily as much as those we have to fight to get.

It is better to travel hopefully than to arrive. (Robert Louis Stevenson)

We all know what other people ought to do to sort out their difficulties – our own are the ones we cannot cope with.

You will see that in themes, the frailty and folly of the human race is often laid bare. This is part of the writer's task: to reveal the reader to himself so skilfully that, as he puts the story down, he smiles a little ruefully and nods. Yes, that's so true. We're only human, all of us.

There is one unbreakable rule about themes and messages, though. Never, never write a story which is completely downbeat and negative. It might well be true that 'we have nothing to look forward to except death' or 'there are no decent human beings, only varying degrees of rotten ones' but readers cannot take utter disillusionment. Certainly editors, who are perhaps the most disillusioned people in the world, will be reluctant to publish anything along these lines.

There are some new writers who feel it is their solemn duty to air humanity's dirty washing, and rub the reader's nose (as it were) in the mess. Such writers are often young, filled with Messianic urgency to rush in where older, more cowardly (they think) writers have trodden with caution. To them, I would say that if utterly negative stories on themes of complete chaos, despair and abandonment have not been published in the past, it is not because those who came before were unaware of the sad state of the world or too timid to mention such things. If certain things were not done, there was probably a very good reason for it. So try to find out what the reason was rather than waste your time making a lot of noise and getting nowhere.

Apart from its message or theme, there is another essential ingredient a short story must possess, and which is an essential part of the plot. There has to be some form of problem or conflict which needs to be overcome by your main character or characters. It is impossible to write a story successfully if it contains no problem, conflict, obstacle or similar set-back which has to be satisfactorily faced up to or worked out by your hero or your heroine.

You may find this difficult to believe. Where is the conflict in a love story? What sort of conflict can there be in a delightful little tale for young children? How can a horror story have obstacles in it? Nevertheless, every good short story not only includes, but is actually based on conflict – conflict that is satisfactorily resolved in order to bring the story to its proper close.

When we speak of conflict, we are not necessarily referring to gun-battles, hand-to-hand fighting, stand-up rows, physical blows. Conflict is often very subtle and may be emotional, verbal or even the agony of a person trying to reach a decision, torn in two by the choice before them. It is on the basis of decisions of this sort that you need to set up your plots.

And here again, the scope appears relatively limited so that new writers are for ever scraping round the bottom of literary barrels trying to invent something completely original which has never been used before. Take my word for it, everything has already been used, but not by you. Have confidence in your own voice, your own view of the world.

I personally was amazed when I realised that other people did not produce the same things I did when we were asked to write on a certain topic at school. This lingered with me for many years, until eventually it sank home that I was given contracts for books and asked to write stories not because I could think of more original things to say than everyone else, but because it was the way (seemingly so obvious to me) that I approached topics like love, death, guilt, ambition, betrayal. Generation after generation of readers remain riveted to stories of love triangles, of struggles to acquire wisdom and maturity, of the fears and spectres that haunt us during the dark hours and the ways in which we try to lay them to rest. The way in which each writer tackles a subject, however well-worn it may be, will give it that special something that makes it fresh and new.

There have been lists compiled of various 'Basic Situations' which, so it is claimed, cover every possible plot there can be. Here are some:

Man against man.
Man against woman.
Man against nature/natural disaster.
Man against the animal kingdom.
Man against himself/his conscience/his religion/his honour.
Man against scientific development.
Man against machine.
Man against the unknown.
Man against injustice/corruption.
Man against a mystery/a puzzle/crime.
Man against emotional entanglement/physical attraction.

You might well be able to think of other situations you could use in a story – the list is only a guide. And once again, you could keep notes to look over in a spare moment, or when you want to try and stir up your brain.

It is worth mentioning at this point – when you are just starting out, on the verge of taking your stories seriously – that many experts advise writers to keep a notebook or a diary and to scribble down impressions, interesting happenings, possible titles, good opening sentences and anything else that might come in useful. It is often hinted that no genuine writer is without the ever-present notebook and pen, and that if you do not keep such a record of your thoughts and ideas, you will never succeed.

In my view, this advice is next door to useless. I have never benefited from keeping a notebook – in the first place because I spent my time trying to get to grips with the actual writing itself, and in the second because all the wonderful titles and ideas I noted down never seemed to fit into what I eventually managed to produce.

Do not regard advice to keep a notebook as something you must follow at all costs. There are equally good reasons why writers should avoid a rag-bag approach of clutter and keep their minds clear to pursue their own lines of thought. Indeed, some would-be writers ostentatiously wave a notebook beneath the noses of family and friends and make a great performance of their note-taking, but apart from filling up a large number of pages, they never seem to progress to the hard graft of actually completing a story.

This is essentially a personal thing. As I have said, I have never kept a notebook and would regard it as a waste of time. You may feel the same, and be secretly relieved that you can go about your writing in your own way without feeling obliged to act out the part of a note-taking would-be author. On the other hand, you may find that you need the physical reassurance of actually making notes, plans, putting your ideas on paper before you proceed further, hoarding snippets of wit and wisdom and other people's thoughts, building up a little library of your own that you can riffle through for inspiration when you need it. So if you want to keep a notebook, do so. If you can see no purpose in it, then don't bother. It is a matter of preference.

SUMMARY

So far we have defined some of the more basic elements that need to be present in a short story. Here they are listed as a convenient reminder.

1. A short story is a piece of prose fiction of variable length.

2. It needs to tell a story, and to have a beginning, middle and end.

3. There can be no story if nothing happens. A story details the events that happen to the characters involved over a chronological period of time.

4. A story must have a message or theme that can be easily and simply summed up. It must tell the reader something about life and living, or human nature.

5. The message is not as important as the fact that it must be presented clearly and well.

6. Avoid at all costs taking a theme which is completely negative and downbeat.

7. A story must be built on some sort of conflict, some obstacle that needs to be overcome, some problem or difficulty that must be sorted out. If there is no conflict, there is no story.

Any fiction should be a story. In any story there are three elements: persons, a situation, and the fact that in the end something has changed. If nothing has changed, it isn't a story.

Malcolm Cowley

6
THE RIGHT
APPROACH

The social and literary revolutions which have taken place during the last half-century – and will probably continue to take place into the immediate future – have changed the traditional concepts of fiction. Traditional ideas of what fiction is, what it means and what writers should be attempting to achieve, have become outdated. They are now, even at best, completely naive and likely to confuse the new writer rather than assist him.

There was a popular conception of the short story writer as an eccentric intellectual whose presence was generally recognised to honour his immediate vicinity; he was regularly requested to declare Garden Fetes open or crown the Rose Queen. The traditional view was that the short story writer was blessed with vocational wisdom and tolerance that raised him above the common herd. Such ideas may still linger, and they do no harm to such onlookers as innocently continue to believe the work of a short story writer to be hallowed by inspirational qualities that mysteriously mark out the writer as an artist giving great things to the world.

The aspiring writer of short stories, however, will do himself no good if he views this as rather a delightful fate and obligingly goes along with such happy little fables. Even worse, it will be disastrous if he actually starts to believe in the role public opinion has cast him, namely that of artist who communes with the muse and thinks a lot, coming up with inspired cameos that impress less intuitive and sensitive readers with his cleverness.

The writer of the past was usually a part-timer of independent means, or someone who dabbled with storywriting in his spare time. It was even possible to make some sort of a career out of this casual and amateur approach. People in the past were satisfied with less, and many a local celebrity built a reputation on a handful of successful submissions to publishers, sometimes even less than that. There was far more of a mystique about the nature of a writer, and what he really did, and the public in general were far less sophisticated and far more gullible.

But today things are very different. These are tough times, and today's writer of fiction – whether of novels or short stories – needs to be a different breed of person altogether. The approach is no longer casual or hit-and-miss. The writer needs to abandon, the sooner the better, all colourful notions of art and the muse. Clear your mind of illusions (temporarily, at any rate) and do not delude yourself that you have any dreams or ambitions so far as your writing goes, other than to make it work, however you have to achieve this.

And what is the approach you need today in order to make it work? Realistically, it is this – that every story ever written was nothing more or less than one great confidence trick. The writer's task is to learn to be a con-man *par excellence*, to learn to put his scam together with skill and flair so that the public at large – including, of course, publishers and editors – do not hesitate but start queuing to put their money on it.

Serious, professional writers have known this for years – it is no secret. But the mystique with which the public has chosen to surround its authors, and often the ignorance of amateur writers who have never really become professionals in their outlook, have tended to obscure the facts. Storywriting is a tough, professional job. Amateurs will fall at the very first fence. And the professionals need to be aware of the fraudulent nature of their work – they are dealing in the hopes and dreams of their readers. It is their job to make readers believe there is joy and love, decency, thoughtfulness, caring, justice and mercy in the world. The facts (which the writer has to bear in mind) indicate that the opposite is probably the case. Nevertheless, any good confidence trickster can put the facts across in such a way that people will believe black is white, dark is light, day is night.

You have got to con your readers into thinking what you want them to think, into believing what you want them to believe and into persuading them that while they are reading your story, it is the only thing they care about in the world.

WHAT SKILLS DOES THE WRITER NEED?

You may already be worrying that you do not possess the skills necessary to make you a successful writer of short stories. Apart from educational skills, you may be thinking, do you have enough awareness and background knowledge about the short story in general? Have you studied the works of classic masters? Etc, etc.

Forget such problems. At this early stage, we have already considered some basic facts we need to know about the short story itself. In this chapter, we will consider the three elements you need to possess (to whatever degree) in order to become a proficient, if not a passably good, writer of short stories.

1. Firstly, you do not need to feel hampered by the lack of a university education or a degree. In many cases, a writer is better off without either. In the same way, you may feel you lack journalistic experience, but it is a fact that a youngster who takes a job as a cub reporter on his local paper, intending to progress to writing short stories or novels, generally remains a reporter for the rest of his working life and never gets as far as the stories.

Once you have become accustomed to writing in a house style, writing a certain way, once you have got into the habit of accepting orders from a tutor or an editor about things you can and cannot do, it is very difficult to break the habit. Consequently, originality of thought and freshness of approach may well be stifled if the writer is employed to 'get the names of the mourners, the messages on the wreaths and the undertaker, nothing else,' or is told that, as a student, he is not allowed to make decisions himself, but has to tabulate the source of every fact or opinion he uses in his writing.

Basically, all the beginner needs is to be able to read and

write, to be able to spell and to have a reasonable working knowledge of grammar. He does not have to be a professor of literature, he can get by with a modestly competent general education and (more important) an alert, enquiring mind and the Writer's Eye we mentioned in the last chapter. He does not have to take *The Times Literary Supplement* or read only works which have been shortlisted for the Booker Prize. Being a good writer is a very different thing from being an intellectual snob – and good writers are often not intellectual at all.

We will be discussing presentation of your work to editors later, but broadly speaking, if you can use any type of typewriter, electronic machine or word-processor – and of course, if you have one at your disposal to make neat, clear copies of what you write – you need not worry about not being properly equipped to make a start on your career.

One other point needs to be made at this stage. It is true that the writer does not need a fully equipped office, he does not need to have letters after his name, he might well have received the greater part of his education at night school. But the prospective writer does need some element of what, for want of a better term, we will call talent.

There are some people, willing to work hard, willing to do anything to succeed, who are lacking in a natural aptitude for writing and who, alas, do not possess even the slightest spark of what we have called talent. For such people – and their lack of talent soon makes itself obvious if they are honest with themselves – I am afraid there is no hope at all. They will save themselves a great deal of heartache if they recognise their lack of potential at an early stage and accept cheerfully the fact that they will never make a writer. If they refuse to do this, they are bringing down the disappointments and hurt that will surely follow on their own head.

As I am certain that you are not one of these unfortunates, but a serious and probably a gifted would-be professional, we can move on to the second group of attributes a writer needs to possess.

2. The writer can get by on the minimum of formal education

and training. He learns to use his Writer's Eye and his own mind to observe the world, and to form his own opinions, conclusions and judgements which he can incorporate into his writing.

However, he does need to be aware of all the skills, techniques and methods he needs in order to be able to put each scam across successfully to his readers and (hopefully) to editors and publishers who will recognise his professionalism and want to buy his work.

These skills are not familiar to the public in general. They are not, as we have seen, necessarily praiseworthy in normal behavioural terms. They are in fact devious, manipulative and crooked. A writer of stories is not bound by the truth – he twists it to suit himself. He is not concerned with morals or respectability, and he does not accept the judgements of society. He uses half-truths, sentimentality, emotive language, even lies, in order to achieve his effects.

As the one person in charge of this whole affair, the writer is classless, he steps outside society to a position of complete power where he alone has his characters in his grasp and can do exactly what he likes with them, pronouncing whatever judgements he will. In his own empire, the writer of stories is a god. His word is law. But what is even more heady is when he succeeds in selling a story to editor and readers. The sense of exhilaration and achievement is something that only another writer who has managed to bring off the same coup can experience and understand.

This is one of the reasons why people aspire to be writers. They want to be up there in the heights, making the rules, in control. And, if you possess the elementary attributes we have already mentioned, and have a degree of talent, you need not worry about how to learn the skills, techniques and tricks of the trade. This book contains all of them.

The writing tricks a writer needs to know are not, in themselves, difficult to learn. They are often new ways of considering aspects of living, of looking at life, rather than actual skills. And because they seem so simple, would-be writers rush past feeling that with a few cursory glances, they have absorbed the technique.

In fact, however, one almost certain rule will apply to everyone who wants to write short stories: you need time to practise. Your first story – I can guarantee – will be a failure (now go on – prove me wrong!). More than likely, your second, third and fourth stories will also be failures. It is at this point that many would-be writers start to grow restless, to flip through *How to Write* manuals wondering where they have gone wrong, to consult with friends to get a second opinion, to decide editors have not given them a fair chance, and so on.

This attitude would be laughable if applied to any other art form. No professional actor rushes through his breathing exercises and voice projection for a whole seven days and then, on the strength of this and one part as a butler (with one line to say) seriously considers playing Lear at Stratford. No student of the piano spends ten minutes a day on cursory practise for six months and then considers himself ready to tackle a professional engagement as a soloist with a great orchestra.

You need to spend time working your apprenticeship as a writer. How long this apprenticeship needs to be will vary with every individual, and you will be reassured to hear that it is not necessarily the length of time spent on practising your storywriting that counts most – it is what you do with that time. But some degree of space for practise, for familiarising yourself with your newly acquired skills, for making the whole thing appear effortless and giving the impression that it just came together with no trouble at all on your part. With the best will in the world, you cannot achieve these things overnight.

Everything you learn, every story or exercise you attempt, even if it is raw and clumsy and does not work out, will nonetheless mark a step forward for you. Nothing a writer ever does is wasted. Nothing you devote time and trouble to will be purposeless, even though you might not feel you are making any progress. I can promise you – you are. Every day, week and month you spend getting to grips with your new career is a day, week or month more of your apprenticeship served and mastered. We all have to go through it. I myself wrote short stories as well as novels from the age of about eight until I made my first sale to *Cycling* magazine with a 1,000 word story, called *Off the Beat!*, about a village policeman. It took me over ten years to work my way to that first acceptance, and the number of failed stories that passed under the bridges in between hardly bear thinking of.

But a child growing up with aspirations of becoming a writer inevitably takes far longer to succeed than an adult who is already basically educated and tackling a new skill in a realistic manner. The most successful new writer I have ever dealt with (a 40-year old lady student whom I tutored for one of the writing correspondence schools) went from being a raw beginner to a monthly contributor to some half dozen magazines, had her first book published and a contract for a second, and a list of over 250 article acceptances – all within the space of three years. Admittedly, she worked harder than the average aspiring writer – but she is not unique. You could do the same, if you are prepared to pursue your goal single-mindedly enough and put in the necessary hours of practise.

The main point that needs to be made here is that you must not expect to become a skilled writer within the space of a few weeks. You must devote the same amount of effort to the task that you would be prepared to give to learning any other art form like painting, dancing, playing an instrument. Give yourself time before you start consulting with friends at the local Writer's Circle and deciding that the editors to whom you have submitted your stories quite obviously do not know their jobs.

3. The third collection of qualities a writer needs must be mentioned here but they will be largely held in reserve for the moment. A sprinkling of talent, the skills for putting across the story – these will get anyone started. But we do have to acknowledge that there are other qualities certain gifted people possess; intuitions, awarenesses, abilities which cannot be pinned down, described or taught. It is in this sense that the cliché arises that writers are born, not made. Great talent, genius, call it what you will, is either there or it isn't. Either way, there is nothing much that can be done to change

the situation.

When writers begin their careers, and even when they become successful, they are seldom able to judge the nature or the depth of their own talent – the greatest storytellers are often those who doubt themselves most, or who are genuinely surprised at the reception their work is given. Katherine Mansfield, for instance, commented in her journal on her classic *The Garden Party* that it 'is a moderately successful story, that is all'.

It is possible that almost anyone who reads this book might be a great writer, one of the special few who can over-step the boundaries of regulations and rules, who can break every proven method of work and yet whose words can hold the reader spellbound, reveal echoing truths that are so filled with compassion, joy, the shining wonders of love and life and even death, that the deep chords from which passion and emotion spring are touched and the reader feels transfigured. Once you have read the work of a really great writer, you are never quite the same person again.

Large numbers of would-be writers have some vague tech-nicolor vision like this in their minds when they take up storywriting, but the worst thing you can possibly do is to start writing with your only aim to exercise this kind of message and present your readers with answers to problems about why we are here, the meaning of life and death and existence and so forth.

It is a fact that even the most humble writer needs to aspire beyond the superficial, and you do need to be aware, however prosaically, of the wonders greatness can accom-plish so that you never lose sight of the shimmering peaks where – if you work hard and are extremely lucky – you might one day arrive at the lowest foothills. Then you can really begin to learn what writing is all about.

But when you start your career as a writer of short stories, avoid dedicating yourself to elevated concepts involving reve-lations of the divine plan, the collective unconscious or Original Sin, philosophy or your own particular theory of the universe. The child begins to read by spelling out *the cat sat on the mat* before he starts investigating the theories of Freud and Darwin, even though the letters and words used in the works of great theorists might be exactly the same as those in his spelling book.

In the same way, anyone starting off as a story writer should ignore (as we are going to do for the time being) the possibility that he might be a genius and the problem of how best to employ his uncommon talents for the benefit of all, including readers who have been starved, as though in a literary desert, of the inspirational truths he is about to impart. One of the first things a real genius has to come to terms with is a sense of his own inadequacy and the frustration of his own limitations. So smash the mirror in which you are admiring your literary profile, get down to the basics and start trying to spell out the short story equivalent of *the cat sat on the mat*, which is where we have all got to start.

SUMMARY

To add to the list we have already made of the basic elements that need to be present in a short story, here is a summary of the ways in which we need to approach the writing of stories, and the elementary skills we require:

1. The writer of today should abandon the rose-tinted spectacles with which authors were inclined to be viewed in the past and accept that writing stories is a tough, skilled profession not to be casually undertaken by amateurs.

2. Every story ever written is a lie from beginning to end, a web of falsehood and deceit, and the writer has to use the tricks of the con-man and professional sharper to persuade the public that more than anything else in the world, it wants to hear this untruthful, fraudulent and quite unrealistic account of events about people who have never existed.

3. More important than any form of higher education, the aspiring writer needs the elements of grammar and spelling, a quick and inquisitive mind and the Writer's Eye. In any situation he may find himself, including in bed with a lover or at

his grandmother's funeral, there will always be a part of his consciousness which is standing metaphorically to one side, taking notes. The writer – for better or for worse – is never off duty, and anyone who cannot understand this concept need read no further.

4. Literature is by no means the same thing as successful story writing, and intellect often has nothing to do with either.

5. However you might long to be a writer, you must accept that you need to possess a certain amount of talent and that if you do not have that magic spark somewhere within you, you are wasting your time. Be realistic. But few people who make serious attempts at becoming writers are completely untalented, so the odds are all in your favour.

6. A writer must approach his work from a viewpoint unconfined by class, rank, sex, age or any other category. He stands outside the law, moral as well as criminal, and is the complete master in his own domain. However, because he has such absolute power, he has to be able to justify everything that happens in his stories and explain away all weaknesses, rough edges, discrepancies, apparent errors of judgement or other faults. This is where his skills as con-man and fluency as a convincing liar come into their own.

7. It is impossible to learn the skills of story writing overnight or even in a few days or weeks. The aspiring writer must spend time and effort in practise in the same way as any other student. Regardless of what you may read or be told anywhere else, there is no short cut to writing skill. But when you consider the benefit your new career will bring you, even if only in satisfaction at your own mastery of the short story form, this is worth taking some time and trouble over. If you could indeed learn this skill overnight – along with every other bored individual who thought it might be fun to become a writer – it would not be worth bothering with, and there would be nothing for you to achieve.

8. Do not start out with a vision of yourself as a literary genius. We all have to start humbly, and even the writers who are literary geniuses are mostly unaware of their special qualities. The characteristics which make up great talent or genius are born in each individual. They cannot be copied, they cannot be taught. Anyone who possesses them will know about it soon enough – and if the Muse passed over you in the queue, do not worry. Most of the rest of the writing fraternity manage to achieve the status of professionals, even if they cannot – and would not in all humility – claim to be among the greats.

There is no denying the fact that writers should be read but not seen. Rarely are they a winsome sight.

Edna Ferber

All fiction for me is a kind of magic and trickery – a confidence trick, trying to make people believe something is true that isn't.

Angus Wilson

7
WHO SINGS THE SONG REBUILDS THE TOWER

We have now reached the point where we can begin to consider the actual writing of our short story, the putting of the words together and the committing of them to paper. It is an awesome task that lies before us. Where do we start? With plot, characters, construction, and all the other technical ingredients? Or even before that with the idea itself, where it is to come from, and the way in which we must handle in order to develop it into a short story successfully?

All of these are skills and techniques the aspiring writer needs to learn, and you may even have your own particular problem – as most beginners do – which causes you especial worry. The list of niggling queries that can confuse and distress the beginner is never ending. How can one tell whether one's idea will make a good short story or whether it would be better as a novel? How exactly is a basic idea developed so that it turns into a story? Where does one get ideas from in the first place? How do you know where to start the story off? And having started, how do you know where to stop? Etc, etc.

Have no fears, we will be dealing with all these queries and many others later in the book. But before we begin to get to grips with the flesh and blood and bones, the structure and content of your story, there is a consideration of vital importance which we must examine even before the story actually comes into existence. This is in fact more relevant than all the technique in the world.

We have seen that the writer must sell his creation to the reader, that he must con the reader into accepting a story unquestioningly. If he is unable to force his reader – by whatever means – into actually reading the narrative, he can never succeed since there will be no communication, no two-way give and take between writer and reader.

A reader (ideally, though often long suffering relatives have no choice in the matter) must be free to make his own decision whether to read a story – because he anticipates that he will obtain pleasure from it – or whether to reject the proffered pages and give the story a miss. Bear this in mind. Too many novice writers are inclined to forget that a story should be a pleasure to the reader, and take the attitude that potential readers who are not impressed by their work and refuse to read it of their own free will, must have it forcibly rammed down their throat. What sort of lover is he who, having failed to seduce, resorts to rape? Never forget that the story writer is there for the benefit of the reader, not the other way about.

So long before the question of whether the story is interesting, skilfully crafted, well characterised and competently written has even been touched upon, before the reader has hardly had a chance to run his eyes over the opening lines, the writer (in his role as confidence trickster, salesman and glib sharper) must catch the reader's interest and convince him that, more than anything, he wants to read this story.

When confronted by a short story, a potential reader makes a psychological decision. If he does not find the prospect of interest, he will dismiss the story, turn the page, and rarely return for a second glance in case his first impression was wrong. In that fraction of a second, the writer has lost him, and it makes not the slightest difference whether the reader has missed the greatest treat of his life. He is not interested in the writer's efforts to please or whether he succeeded or not. The writer never has a chance to justify himself, to plead his case, to make explanations. His story must stand or fall on its own merits, and if the reader does not think it looks worth reading, he will not read it.

If the reader decides to read the story, however, he makes an intellectual commitment to it, and even if he does not find it as enjoyable as he had expected, he will probably (unless extremely provoked) read it to the end and then say to whoever is nearby that he thought it was a load of rubbish. But whatever his reaction afterwards, he has read your story and you have had the opportunity to work your 'scam' on him. It is in these preliminary moments rather than in all your delicacy of description, wonderful use of colour and light and shade, illumination of personality, that you will lay the foundations for your success as a story writer.

So exactly what is involved in hooking a reader so that he is unable to pass your story by? How do you catch his attention and hold it? The answer is made up of a complex bundle of items which are often proffered in well-intentioned but not entirely clear advice to writers like: 'Make sure your story has an irresistible opening line' or 'Plunge straight in, start the story moving'. Before we examine this in more detail, however, I want you to consider the following openings of stories, some by classic writers, others more humbly written, from all historical periods and parts of the world.

They are immensely varied in style and subject, but they have two things in common. They have been successful as short stories (obviously to different degrees) – and they all possess the glue-like quality that will draw a reader's eye and keep it riveted to the page. I defy anyone to feel his attention straying after a paragraph with any of these. If there was a guarantee of reader-friendly, all of these would carry the stamp.

In order for us to appreciate that it is not the time, place, subject or any other unifying quality which gives a story an irresistible grip on the reader, these examples are given anonymously here, but listed together with their authors at the end of the chapter. See whether you can spot just what it is about them that grabs and retains your interest in only a few lines.

READER-FRIENDLY OPENING LINES

1. Of an early evening when there is nothing much doing anywhere else, I go around to Good Time Charley's little speak in West Forty-seventh Street that he calls the Gingham Shoppe, and play a little klob with Charley, because business is quiet in the Gingham Shoppe at such an hour, and Charley gets very lonesome.

He once had a much livelier spot in Forty-eighth Street that he called the Crystal Room, but one night a bunch of G-guys step into the joint and bust it wide open, besides confiscating all of Charley's stock of merchandise. It seems that these G-guys are members of a squad that comes on from Washington, and being strangers in the city they do not know that Good Time Charley's joint is not supposed to be busted up, so they go ahead and bust it, just the same as if it is any other joint.

2. George Pickard, with a sickening start, woke for the fifth time in a month from a strange dream of his father, who had died suddenly six weeks before.

As always in the dream, his father was catching a train. It was midwinter and bitterly cold and the train, as always, was the night express to the north: sleeper coaches with drawn blinds, white steam from two big engines curdling into a black freezing sky, a strong air of suspense under the hooded yellow lights of an almost deserted platform No. 3.

3. Aunt Amy was out on the front porch, rocking back and forth in the high-backed chair and fanning herself, when Bill Soames rode his bicycle up the road and stopped in front of the house.

Perspiring under the afternoon 'sun', Bill lifted the box of groceries out of the big basket over the front wheel of the bike, and came up the front path.

Little Anthony was sitting on the lawn, playing with a rat. He had caught the rat down in the basement – he had made it think that it smelled cheese, the most rich-smelling and crumbly-delicious cheese a rat had ever thought it smelled, and it had come out of its hole, and now Anthony had caught hold of it with his mind and was making it do tricks.

4. 'Don't look now,' John said to his wife, 'but there are a couple of old girls two tables away who are trying to hypnotise me.'

Laura, quick on cue, made an elaborate pretence of yawning, then tilted her head as though searching the skies for a non-existent aeroplane.

'Right behind you,' he added. 'That's why you can't turn round at once – it would be much too obvious.'

Laura played the oldest trick in the world and dropped her napkin, then bent to scrabble for it under her feet, sending a shooting glance over her left shoulder as she straightened once again. She sucked in her cheeks, the first tell-tale sign of suppressed hysteria, and lowered her head.

'They're not old girls at all,' she said. 'They're male twins in drag.'

5. Coal all spent; the bucket empty; the shovel useless; the stove breathing out cold; the room freezing; the leaves outside the window rigid, covered with rime; the sky a silver shield against any one who looks for help from it. I must have coal; I cannot freeze to death; behind me is the pitiless stove, before me the pitiless sky, so I must ride out between them and on my journey seek aid from the coal-dealer. But he has already grown deaf to ordinary appeals; I must prove irrefutably to him that I have not a single grain of coal left, and that he means to me the very sun in the firmament.

6. While I was waiting for you in the foyer of that superb hotel, I started talking with the head porter. Once, during the time when we were getting engaged, you said to me:

'I think you talk to people – strangers – for a funny reason: not because you really want to, but as if you had to prove that you can make friends with anyone.'

This was one of your more acute comments, sweetheart; there is some kind of back-handed conceit which prompts this habit of mine. But it really sprang originally from my being rather undersized and shy when I was younger...

7. It was already Thursday when Deidre left her grave. The rain had made the soil soft and the loam clung to her cerements like a distracted lover. It was so late, the night so sodden, that there was no-one to see her as she left the manicured lawns and chaste marble stones behind her for the enticing litter of the city.

'Pardon me, miss.' The night-watchman was old, white-haired under his battered hat. He held the flashlight aimed at her face, seeing only a dishevelled young woman with mud in her hair, a wild look about her eyes, a livid cast to her face like a bruise. He wondered if she had been attacked; there was so much of that happening these days. 'You all right, miss?'

8. 'Derek will die,' pronounced Miss Brood, and when Derek duly expired, in a flurry of feathers at the bottom of his cage, she was not surprised. Clairvoyance was her gift. Doom was her speciality.

'I shall never find a husband,' said Miss Brood.

'You're a pessimist,' said the cheerful, trainee social worker who came to see why she lived alone.

'No, I shall never find a husband.' Miss Brood expelled a withered sigh. Then she trembled, had one of her presentiments and added sadly, 'And you'll fail your exams.'

'You're a pessimist!' asserted the social worker.

But she failed her exams.

FIRST CATCH YOUR READER

Basically, the initial impact any story makes on a potential reader consists of two things: the personality of the narrator who is telling the story (whether this is one of the characters taking part, or the author himself) and the credibility and authenticity of the world into which he finds himself transported.

It has to be admitted that not every good – or even great – short story begins charismatically. Some, going by the standards we have just set, have extremely poor openings and the reader has to make a real effort to get going. But because writers might have got away with boring beginnings in the past, that is no excuse to be slipshod about your own. It is vital to be aware of the impact, based on the two points outlined above, which matter more than anything else about your story when the reader first picks up your manuscript.

So first, let us examine the role played by the narrator, the character, voice, personality or whatever else you like to call it which speaks directly to the reader when he begins to read. It might give us a good deal of useful information if we could consider the faults of those narrators who *fail* to grip their readers. But this important point can rarely be examined by new writers since they have little or no chance to read badly-written and otherwise amateurish stories with the intention of comparing the failures with those which are successful.

If you were able to do this, however, you would find that most stories which do not hold your attention (or anybody's attention) seem to be narrated by a colourless, insubstantial, boring, twittering sort of person with a thin and unconvincing voice and presence. Such narrators do not seem to be very sure what they are talking about; sometimes they speak very loudly with grimly clenched teeth (as it were) in order to ram their point home. However they seem to need to peer surreptitiously at cue-cards clasped in their hands in order to clarify exactly what their point is.

Any sign of uncertainty or confusion, too profuse explanations and repetition, too much filling in of unnecessary background or brightly artificial acting out of the scene in order to try and hustle the reader into the picture – all these are doomed to fail. And they fail because the writer was not aware of the role which the narrator of any short story must play.

He is not there just to fill in the gaps, to give prologues and epilogues, to underline or explain odd points, to carry the reader over awkward bits. Great stories – like those above – always grip the reader because they are told by a narrator who accompanies the reader every step of the way. He knows the story he has to tell without reference to any notes or cue-cards; he is intimately familiar with it and speaks with an authority that is genuine, unforced and carries complete conviction. Because of this, the reader is unable to resist the lure of his narrative.

So point one: it is essential in order to grip your reader, for you to be on clear and familiar terms with your story and all the events and people in it. There must be nothing you are not sure about. This ring of authority in the narrator's voice is the first step towards grabbing your reader.

The second is that the narrator must know his way round, be at ease, be at home in the world in which he finds himself, and be utterly familiar with every part of it.

It is commonly believed by new writers that a story is built up from the outside, like a house of cards. One is placed here, another there, a detail about this or that character is filled in, an incident here or there will flesh the story out. When his house of cards is completed, the writer proceeds triumphantly to conduct his reader in and out of the rooms and around the environs of his fabricated landscape.

But the whole point about a successful story is that the reader must not feel, consciously or unconsciously, that he is stepping out of reality into some sort of artificial other-world. Look back at the openings listed above. Did any of them give that impression? Indeed not – every reader caught up in those openings would have felt he was stepping into a reality more gripping, more interesting, more thrilling than any ordinary everyday reality could possibly be.

The reader must actually feel that he is stepping into a true reality rather than out of it when he begins to read a short story, and during the time he is reading, the story must be more real to him than anything in his own world. Technical ploys like plot, character, description, have nothing to do with this utter absorption – it is the quiet, gripping voice of the narrator and the authenticity of the world into which he has been transported that will hold the reader fast.

THE SONG AND THE TOWER

When you sit down to write a story – whether it is your first or your hundred and first – you are not just undertaking an exercise in stringing words together. The art of storytelling is something as old as our civilization itself, indeed older, since it reaches back to the very dawn of time. When the barely literate cavemen sat round their fires in the frighteningly dark dangerous night, there was always, somewhere, a voice in the background. Perhaps it emitted only a few grunts, but it conjured up for them the ritual charms, the magic formulae, the reliving of the exploits of their heroes and those who had passed before and who had reached out to touch the sky, to brave the other side of the mountain or kill the legendary great beast.

Held by the power of that voice, its authority, and the wonders of the world into which the storyteller transported them, primitive men would sit silent, flesh creeping with unspoken emotion. They would be temporarily blinded to the leaping firelight and the smothering darkness that made up reality, clutching to their breasts the colour and the magic of the spell the storyteller's voice was weaving.

And every writer who today tells a story is carrying on the tradition of this ancient, honourable and mysterious craft. He is providing food for the reader's soul, giving him inner sustenance. Perhaps your story is not about heroes and charms and wonders in the accepted sense. That does not matter. Why do people read at all, when they are perfectly aware that what they are reading is a pack of lies? What do they expect to gain from perusing a story – and what does it, in fact, give them?

The answer to this is that the reality of the storyteller's imaginative recreation of the world, how he sees it and what he perceives to be the truth embodied in his story, can open the reader's eyes to aspects of life and living, of people and their relationships, of which he was not aware. We have already quoted Anaïs Nin as saying: 'It is the function of art to renew our perception... The writer shakes up the familiar scene, and as if by magic, we see a new meaning in it.'

By keeping this aspect of our craft at the back of our minds, we will automatically assist ourselves to bring a sense of authority to our narrator and a convincing reality to our story. And by keeping faith with what we hold to be precious, valuable, good and true as we 'sing our song', we will help in the rebuilding of the soaring tower of inner fantasy and vision which can so often crumble beneath the vanity, bored commercialism and poor quality efforts of writers who have perhaps made their name, and no longer need to try any more. To some extent, they can get away with less than the best.

Remember that voice in the dark, charming the fears of the

night away by creating new realities beside those primitive fires, and take that ancient storyteller as your example as you tackle your own stories.

Reader-Friendly Stories

Below are the titles of the stories given as examples earlier. Try to read them if you can. Many of them are classics in their fields and can be found in short story collections. As you progress, read as many short stories as possible, of whatever sort. Try to cultivate a critical sense so that you begin to recognise whether a story is good, and if so, why – or if not, why not. Apply all the technical tests we will be considering to the stories you read, and turn them inside out. If they are good stories, they will be able to stand such cavalier treatment and still remain good when you have finished.

1. *Dream Street Rose* by Damon Runyon.
2. *The Ring of Truth* by H.E. Bates.
3. *It's a Good Life* by Jerome Bixby.
4. *Don't Look Now* by Daphne du Maurier.
5. *The Bucket Rider* by Franz Kafka.
6. *Leave Cancelled* by Nicholas Monsarrat.
7. *Disturb Not My Slumbering Fair* by Chelsea Quinn Yarbro.
8. *Miss Brood's Speciality* by Roger F. Dunkley.

Summary

Continuing our list of easy points of reference which have been touched on in this chapter:

1. Even before the many and varied aspects of technique come to be considered when approaching a story, the writer must bear in mind that the first important thing he needs to do is to persuade the reader to read it.

2. The reader will make a choice when he picks up a book or magazine. If he does not think a story looks interesting, he

will pass over it. The writer must convince him he wants to make the commitment to read it. Only in this way can the writer communicate and work on the reader with all the subtleties of his scam and skill.

3. Storytelling is an ancient art, and has kept man enthralled for centuries because of the power and authority of the storyteller and his ability to transport his listeners into a world which is more real to them than their own everyday reality.

4. A storyteller who has this authority and sense of reality will draw the reader irresistibly into his story from his very first words.

5. A sense of truth and values will assist in the storyteller's art and add richness to the story's effect on the reader.

A tale charms by its ingenuity, by the plausibility with which it overcomes the suspicion that it couldn't happen. That is art.

Jacques Barzun

The natural habit of any good and critical reader is to disbelieve what you are telling him and try to escape out of the world you are picturing.

Angus Wilson

A great writer creates a world of his own and his readers are proud to live in it. A lesser writer may entice them in for a moment, but soon he will watch them filing out.

Cyril Connolly

PART III
PRACTICAL TECHNIQUES OF STORY WRITING

8
THE BASIC IDEA

Authors – essayist, atheist, novelist,
*   realist, rhymester, play your part,*
Paint the mortal shame of nature
*   with living hues of Art.*
Rip your brothers' vices open, strip
*   your own foul passions bare;*
Down with Reticence, down with Reverence –
*   forward – naked – let them stare.*
                              Alfred, Lord Tennyson.

Many new writers are frightened at the thought of how they are going to find an idea for their story. It seems, they think, to have something to do with 'getting inspiration'. But where does inspiration come from? Not being familiar with this mysterious element, they do not quite know what to expect. Does one just sit back and wait for inspiration? How will they know if and when it has arrived? And what if nothing happens and inspiration does not come up with anything suitable? The page before them is a blank, and they begin to panic. Just how does a writer get started?

Ask the greats, and they may well be flippant about this important point. 'Writing is easy,' says Gene Fowler, 'all you do is sit staring at a blank sheet of paper until the drops of blood form on your forehead.' Red Smith adds cheerfully: 'There's nothing to writing. All you do is sit down at a type-writer and open a vein.'

This joking attitude, however, covers up the genuine concern which even very experienced writers can feel for this aspect of their work. There is no easy answer to the question of where ideas come from. They are part of the mysterious processes of creation which are worked out in the depths of the mind's subconscious. A great deal of what happens during the creation of a story takes place in the dark, out of our reach, and outside our control. There are times when we might be aware of the subconscious and conscious parts of our mind overlapping, and these produce 'rules' which all experienced writers know are true, even though they are largely intuitive.

For instance, brilliant ideas, working out of plots and exciting new developments might well come to a writer in his sleep, in dreams or in some semi-waking state. 'You never have to change anything you got up in the middle of the night to write,' declares Saul Bellow, and all experienced professional authors know this is true. But they would find it difficult to explain exactly how the process works. We have to take much of the creative process on trust.

In the words of Ralph Waldo Emerson: 'All writing comes by the grace of God.'

On a more prosaic level, however, you will be happy to hear that, by and large, you can forget about inspiration and stop waiting for it to bring you the answers you are seeking. We have it on good authority that inspiration in the form in which it is popularly envisaged, does not exist. In fact, it *is* still there, but it is not what newcomers commonly imagine it to be – a sort of lightning bolt which makes the recipient cry 'Eureka!' as all becomes crystal clear, and gets him started frantically writing.

Francoise Sagan tells us that 'Writing is just having a sheet of paper, a pen and not a shadow of an idea of what you're going to say.' Stephen Leacock assures us wryly: 'Writing is no trouble: you just jot down ideas as they occur to you. The jotting is simplicity in itself – it is the occurring which is difficult.' And as E.M. Forster remarks cryptically: 'How do I know what I think until I see what I say?'

Good stories are the result of a lot of technical labour rather than sudden bolts from the blue. They are not gifts which float down from the clouds on the wings of artistic inspiration, complete and fully-formed. They are more like relatively formless masses of material which have to be painstakingly worked into shape by the writer. In some respects, a writer has a good deal in common with a sculptor who has to form the figure that he sees in his mind's eye from a lump of clay.

I once read (or it might have been that I misinterpreted) a remark by Truman Capote concerning talent which makes a lot of sense: that the basic idea for a story is like the tiny irritant which lodges inside an oyster and proceeds to form a pearl. The idea can come from anywhere, and it can range from a single glimpse, flash of vision, sense of character, specific scene, to somebody's life story. Anything at all whether true or completely imaginary, whether it makes sense or not, whether it is something as far removed from fiction and short stories as an old cookery recipe, a newspaper item, the spell a woman can cast on Midsummer Eve to conjure up the face of her future husband – absolutely anything that stirs your brain to working and lingers there, refusing to leave you alone until you do something to turn it into a short story, can give you your basic idea.

Look around you. Everywhere, there are potential 'irritants' which might precipitate the beginning of that forming of the pearl. It could be something you see, hear, feel, a face that catches your attention, the way two people are behaving, a dog running to his master, worship in his eyes. In all probability, it will be something quite trivial. Do not worry yourself silly looking for amazing and incredible ideas. Stories are, mainly, about relatively ordinary characters the reader can identify with, not supermen and women.

Some everyday scene or event might well strike the spark – ideas are all around you, swarming in on you. Remember the lists we made of what we could see, hear and feel with our senses using our Writer's Eye earlier?

Here is just one example of something unremarkable that could well lodge in your brain and begin its work. Perhaps, passing in a bus or car, you catch a glimpse of a single lovely gown in the window of an exclusive bridal shop. There is no face beneath the cloud of tulle above it, and only the false hands of the model hold the posy of tightly curled Victorian rosebuds. Somehow, though, there is something about the glimpse you have had which hovers in your mind and seems to haunt you so that at the most unexpected times, like when you are having a bath or cutting your toe nails, you find the vision of the gown swimming before your inner vision, waiting.

Is it the dress itself that has fired your imagination? Surely not – there is nothing unusual or different about a beautiful wedding gown. Is it the woman who created the dress? No, for she has done her part and seems to have disappeared into the background. Then is it the woman who will wear that lovely creation? The faceless woman whose stiff hands will hold the posy of Victorian roses?

Now, what on earth has encouraged us to use those emotive words – 'faceless', 'stiff hands'? Almost as though the bride who will wear that lovely dress is going to be – dead?

But that is impossible – how could she be dead at her wedding? Somebody would be sure (at the very least!) to notice. No, it is not so much the actual wedding – and this is where our brain actually begins to engage the gears of our story after the preliminary work. The story itself will be about the society photographer who took the wedding pictures – he will be our central character. And the story starts when he is developing the film. To his consternation, he finds that the bride's face seems to be in deep shadow on each picture – almost as though it was not there at all. And her hands seem to be marked, streaked somehow with dark patches so that they look crumbly. Her rose pink varnished nails seem to stand out obscenely like stage props stuck onto a clay model.

What is he to do? He is sure there is something badly wrong, and not just a routine accident to the film. The newly married couple are honeymooning at the bridegroom's country house in Suffolk. Our hero decides to pay them a call... and then? Well, you might like to try your new wings out on this one. See what you can do with it.

It is likely that beginners to storywriting might need to force their ideas to start with – create an artificial irritant to think about and ponder on – since as we have already seen, the techniques need a lot of practise. So if no little spark, no face, idea, question, theory, story or any other irritant will lodge in your brain and refuse to leave you alone, create one for yourself at random and make an exercise of concentrating and working on it. In due course, you will find that the genuine article will begin to slide into your mind of its own accord.

Once the speck of dirt, the particle of sand or whatever, has entered the oyster, the pearl begins to form around it. It may take a long time. In the same way, once an idea – a mere glimpse at present, shapeless, formless, just something that keeps nagging at your brain – has lodged itself in your mind, the process of creating your story is under way.

It is at this point that inspiration might well enter the picture. But what exactly will it do to help you get your act together and your story on the road? Let us hear what some more of the experts think on this subject.

'Inspiration,' declares Stanley Elkin, 'is a sort of spontaneous combustion – the oily rags of the head and the heart.' While Doris Lessing says briskly: 'I've always disliked words like *inspiration*. Writing is probably like a scientist thinking about some scientific problem, or an engineer about an engineering problem.'

In other words, once the irritant of whatever sort is lodged in the writer's brain, what happens next is a combination of developments from the subconscious, over which the writer has little control – and hard work of the sort that a professional writer becomes used to, on a severely technical and practical level.

The idea, thought, flash of interest or whatever prompted your story in the first place, rarely if ever arrives in the shape of a short story itself. But once you have your basic concept, you can get to work to create something from it which will fulfil the requirements of the short story form. You can build round it, develop it, narrow it down, tighten it or otherwise provide whatever licks it needs to pull it into shape.

It is worth bearing in mind that often, the shortening, cutting or tightening process will be far more necessary than elaboration or adding on. Say, for instance, that your irritant involves the tale of a cosmetic surgeon who is given the power of healing hands in a deal with the devil, so that he

71

becomes world famous. But under the terms of his diabolical bargain, he is only allowed to use his skill to make money for his own material pleasures. Then one day, he is called to operate urgently on a young nun who has been burned trying to save two children from a fire –. Crisis! What happens next?

What, indeed? There is the making of a gripping short story here, but also, since the story reaches back to the young man's first encounter with the devil and the bargain struck between them – possibly even to his childhood ambition to be rich, or famous, or both – it may be difficult to differentiate between this story's potential as a novel or as a short story.

The author Joyce Carol Oates is on record within comparatively recent years as declaring that: 'I believe that any short story can become a novel, and any novel can be converted back into a short story or into a poem.'

In spite of backing-up comments like Ambrose Bierce's definition of a novel as 'A short story padded', this comment is misleading and even dangerous. The underlying principle is sound enough, but the words themselves, especially when earnestly applied to their own work by beginners, simply do not work. Never try to cram a potential novel into a short story, or pad out the pages of a novel with material which should by rights have fitted comfortably into just a few thousand words. The nature of the novel and the short story are entirely different, and you cannot interchange them.

In 1950, a revised and enlarged edition of a book called *Short Stories: How To Write Them* was published by Herbert Jenkins. Its author was Cecil Hunt, whose qualifications included the fact that he had formerly been fiction editor of *The Daily Mail* and *The Evening News* and literary editor of *The Daily Mail*. And this in the glorious days when most newspapers, as well as many periodicals long since folded, carried regular short stories as a matter of course. Not only that, the standard was, it was taken for granted, of the highest.

Cecil Hunt – along with many other authorities including myself – does not go along with Ms Oates' opinion quoted above. His pithy comments about the difference between the novel and the short story are fascinating, and just as applicable today as they were when he wrote them. He was one of the professional newspapermen who had spent a lifetime in the business, and whose book was endorsed in glowing terms on the dust jacket by writers like Gilbert Frankau and Compton MacKenzie. Let us hear what he had to say:

'The most misleading fault is to believe that the short story is a condensed novel, or even the skeleton of a novel.

'If it were possible to look at a full-length novel through the wrong end of a telescope, the result would not be a short story. It would be a panorama so packed that almost all the detail would be lost. The scene would be too crowded for anything to be appreciated, for any character to move freely or to be understood.

'Perhaps the nearest comparison that will help the beginner is to call the novel a picture and a short story a cameo.

'The short story must confine itself to an incident or group of incidents that would be only 'incidental' in a novel. That does not mean a short story cannot be based on a *motive* that could well form the theme of a novel, but in the short story only a comparatively small incident or phase can be successfully used to illustrate the motive and to prove the point.'

'... Whole lives, whole generations, whole countries, whole continents, can be covered in a novel. A short story must be as compact as possible – characters reduced to the minimum; situation, time, and action all concentrated and clean-cut.

'Remember that, compared with the ten-gallon tank of the novel, the short story is a pint pot. The consummate artist may so husband his treasures, so express their delights, that we may derive more joy from ten minutes with the pint pot than we should secure by drawing of the ten-gallon tank every evening for six weeks – *but the former receptacle is still a pint pot, holding no more and advisedly no less.*

'Overcrowding, then, is a deadly sin in short-story writing. It applies not only to characters, but to the questions of time and place. Keep these as compact as possible.'

It is worth noting that the ideas you are likely to become absorbed with, the incidents, themes and situations which will attract your interest, will spring from a recognisable well of material. This, your own special source of material, will influence everything you write. In whatever convoluted and disguised a form, it will be there somewhere.

You have no choice over your subject matter and the things which will burst out of your writing, and you cannot make a conscious decision to follow up any particular source. For what you write will be almost entirely drawn from your own life, particularly the early years. All the great writers are in agreement on this. Willa Cather says: 'Most of the basic material a writer works with is acquired before the age of fifteen', while Ignazio Silone claims that 'No one can ever write about anything that happened to him after he was twelve years old'.

Often, a writer will explore the same topic, the same problem or burning interest which, without his awareness, pervades everything he sets down on paper. Let us hear how Andre Maurois puts it: 'Almost all the great writers have as their motif, more or less disguised, the "passage from child-hood to maturity", the clash between the thrill of expecta-tion, and the disillusioning knowledge of the truth. *Lost Illusion* is the undisclosed title of every novel'.

Other writers have expressed the same theory, and at one time, I found this not only a boring thought, but difficult to believe. Surely, if one was writing about the same thing all the time, the stories would all be the same, and the re-hashing of that particular subject would stand out a mile? But, many years into my own career when I had acquired a little wisdom, I began to examine my own work.

I found the result staggering. From the children's stories I had written in the days when I supplied newspapers with a weekly column, through all my adult stories, the humorous as well as the serious, and even including my novels and plays, I discovered there has been one deeply hidden, but definite thread running through every single piece of fiction I have ever written, almost without exception. My theme, the preoccupation of my own particular mind, which is obviously still being debated at great length in the depths of my subconscious, since the various parts of my brain do not appear to have come up with the answer, is the struggle of the personality to find its own identity.

In case you think this means my stories must all be rather intellectual and traumatic, I will cite, as one of the ways in which this theme varied itself – without my conscious knowledge, of course – the story of *Theo, The Tubby Teddy*, who tried hard to slim so that his young master would think better of him. Poor Theo had all but given up and resigned himself to being fat, when his master snuggled up to him in bed, telling him how Theo's cuddliness comforted him, and how glad he was that his dear old tubby friend was there.

Another children's story concerned the ambitions of Dalrymple, a young dragon who did not care for dragon-like pursuits, and who even disgraced the family by falling asleep during an exhibition of dragon-roaring and fire-breathing. Dalrymple desperately wanted to be an actor, or even to get into films. In the end, he found his niche when his efforts resulted in his being photographed as the model for the dragon on the flag of Wales! Fame at last!

A third story (not for children) featured the problems of a Thirties ghost (who looked like Carole Lombard) and her disillusionment with her profession. How could she expect to be taken seriously when even traditional phantoms like the Headless Lady and the Black Monk were finding it difficult to make a living? In the end, she decided to take up the amorous propositions of a man who saw her as nothing but a lovely body and face, cash in on her assets and let the haunting go hang!

I was stunned when it came home to me that, without my being aware of it, I had been writing for years on the same subject, and was probably unable to tackle any other subject even if I made a conscious effort. But this experience of mine does illustrate that no one need feel limited or restricted because they have not travelled widely or met interesting people, ridden a mule through the Grand Canyon or been serenaded in a gondola in Venice.

If you are having problems with your own work, and seem unsure which way to go, it might very well help you if you are aware – to a limited extent: do not start psychoanalysing your work or you will come to a jarring halt – of your own particular preoccupations. But do not expect signposts immediately to appear pointing you in the right direction. What you will probably find is that, when confronted with a certain idea or topic, or trying to write one particular story, you feel uneasy with it but do not know why. In all probability, you have wandered from your own personal territory and have strayed from your motif. The best thing to do in such a case is to abandon it and start another.

SUMMARY

1. Stories are created largely in the subconscious by processes which are intuitive. Writers can sometimes find themselves in touch with their subconscious in a semi-waking state, or in sleep or dreams.

2. Stories come into being through hard work on the author's part rather than inspiration. The sort of inspiration that is popularly believed to arrive in an author's mind with the story complete and fully fashioned does not exist.

3. The story is formed in the same way as a pearl forms inside an oyster. The original irritant that sets the process in motion within the author's mind can come from anywhere, at any time, without the author's volition, and can be a single glimpse or idea, line of dialogue or part of a scene – or a complete life history.

4. The original irritant will probably be relatively trivial, and potential irritants that could spark off stories are all around

the author in his everyday life, just waiting.

5. Beginners and inexperienced writers may not find the process easy at first, and may need to force their ideas by consciously creating an irritant and then working on it. With practise, the genuine germs of stories will come of their own accord.

6. The writer must work on the embryo story in a technical and practical way, using his skills to develop the idea, shape it, and often cut it drastically to its basics.

7. A short story is not the same as a novel, and the two cannot be interchanged. Different ingredients go to make up each and while a novel covers a wide canvas a story must be kept compact and as economical as possible. It will only be able to cover one or two incidents which might have made up a relatively tiny part of a novel. A story is concentrated, every word, every detail has to play its part.

8. A writer generally uses as his material the events, incidents and experiences of his early life and often explores similar themes in all his work. If he does wander into relatively unfamiliar territory, he may find the going difficult and not know why. It helps to be aware of your own particular limitations.

9
WHERE TO BEGIN

'I was born in Cambridge just before the Second World War, and since my father was to be killed at Dunkirk, my mother had a struggle to bring myself and my brother up alone. We often went to visit my Granny in London, and I found that by the time I was about ten, I had decided I did not like the south, consequently, when I came to choose a university to apply for, I wanted to go to Edinburgh, and was lucky enough to get a place.'

This is an example of one place where the writer does *not* begin his story. Generally, anything that sounds as though it is the start of a CV or as if the central character is writing his or her memoirs belongs in a novel rather than a story (and even there, it needs to be a great deal more interesting than a bald recital of facts).

The exception might be if the date of the writer's birth has some important bearing on the tale, and plays a part in it. For instance the following is very different to the example above:

'I was fifteen in the year of Waterloo, the child of war, and it might be said that the star in my ascendant which was to blaze across my life chart was not only the fiery Mars but the person of Napoleon Bonaparte. He was to be my one, my only lover, brought to my arms from the blood and smoke of campaigns and battle strategies, of cannon and torn banners and the humiliation of defeat.'

It is important that, though you realise your story must have a good, arresting beginning, you do not worry too much about it just at present. Remember that when a writer begins his story, he does not know exactly what the finished product will be like. Until you have your story actually written – in some form, even if only in a first draft that needs working on

– a work of art complete in itself, you cannot make any real attempt to smooth out all the wrinkles. All the smoothing and polishing is done later, when the basic task of bringing the story into existence on the page has been got out of the way and refinements can be made to knock the corners off and smooth the jagged edges.

So for the time being, allow yourself to start your story at any point you like, even, if you feel so inclined at 'I was born in' – but bear in mind that you are almost certainly going to have to come back afterwards to do some tidying up.

Most beginner writers need to 'write themselves into' a story, and may ramble on for several pages before they actually get down to the nitty gritty of what they are really trying to say. In fact, you may like to bear in mind when you come back to revise your own work, that a useful tip from professional editors is that when cutting or subbing prose written by beginners, it is generally taken for granted that the opening paragraph/s will almost always need to come out.

Often, the opening paragraph – or even the opening page or two – is used by the writer (completely unaware, of course) as a sort of jumping off which he needs to get him going, but which is completely unnecessary to the story. But if you worry yourself sick about this, you will never get started, so spread yourself out as much as you like, avoiding self-criticism and waiting until you have reached the end before you come back to try and decide whether your 'opening sentence' is actually half-way down page two. If it is, scrap the original opening and start the story then and there. You may find you do not seem to learn your lesson and continue to practise this procedure with every story you write, but so long as you are able to cut out the irrelevant bits afterwards when you are doing your revision, do not worry. If you need to write yourself in, do it – but just make sure you cut out your springboard afterwards.

Beginnings are important not only because they must capture the interest of the reader, but because they can affect the actual shape of the story. Start in the wrong place, hit off on the wrong foot, and the whole thing limps along as a result without ever being able to put itself right.

Let us examine how a short story takes on its shape. The action – the plot, which we will be considering later – can usually be summed up in a sentence or two (unlike a novel, which takes several hundred pages to narrate). 'Boy meets girl, they hate each other, until they realise that the violent emotion they feel is really love and they blissfully contemplate a lifetime of squabbling together.'

'A woman discovers she has been sacrificing herself to husband and family for years, quite unnecessarily, since they feel she smothers them, and she is able to break away with their help to live her own life to the full.' 'Criminal thinks he has got away with his crime, but police inspector traps him on a small detail which the criminal's great brain had thought too insignificant to bother about.'

You will see that each of these – and indeed, any other short story you like to examine – is concerned with some sort of turning point, some sort of crisis. Occasionally the crisis in a short story can mark a dramatic change in the lives of the characters, but more often, especially in popular fiction (as opposed to great literature – though this can be extremely subtle) the crisis – or what is often referred to as the climax – indicates only a change in outlook over relatively minor details.

Somebody who has been frustrated and resentful suddenly sees how lucky they really are, and counts their blessings instead of crying for the moon. Or a woman who has felt herself to be useless is made aware of her valued contribution to life, from a completely unexpected quarter.

It is important to be clear about the crisis and the climax. In a short story, the climax is what the whole story builds up to; it is the resolution of the conflict the story has embodied, and marks the end of the struggle or developing situation with which the whole story has involved itself. In this sense, the climax is something highly artificial, as much a part of the carpentry of putting a story together as consciously being aware of the way the tensions build up and the dialogue reveals character. A climax, as it happens in a short story, never takes place in real life. It is far too contrived.

The crisis, on the other hand, is something that the reader

assumes to have been building up in the lives of the characters he is reading about, since they were born. If those characters were real people, they would have lived a whole
lifetime in relative anonymity until the moment of crisis
dawned and the story in which they were going to play the
leading roles began to act itself out.

You will see, therefore, that each short story must begin
when the moment of crisis for the central character is at hand
and events are beginning the build-up to what will ideally
prove to be both the crisis, the turning point for that character, and the climax of the story.

Writers – especially of short stories – are not generally in
the habit of picking up and putting down the same set of
characters repeatedly. If your central character is a dear old
grandmother called Lily, whose clear sighted country wisdom
is going to prove more valuable than book learning when
problems in living have to be overcome, the climax of your
story will come when Lily's home truths prove themselves
and a problem that was looming is solved.

You could say that Lily's whole life will have been lived
with the solving of that particular problem in mind, and once
she has played her part you will put the story to one side and
think about the next one. You are not likely to consider other
situations with Lily in her teens or her twenties, where she is
in the process of developing her amazing home-spun wisdom.

Characters in stories are, in this sense, disposable. They
may be heart-wrenching, utterly memorable, but once they
have done what you want them to, gone through the crisis
you have, as it were, bred them for, then they can be
discarded. Their usefulness is at an end.

In this light, you will see that this is what gives fictional
people both their artistic unreality and their impression on
the reader of being more real than your next door neigh-
bours. Fictional people rarely have more than a few concerns
in life, and they think in only two or three directions. In this
way, their passionate preoccupation with their in-laws, or
their boy friend or whatever their crisis will be linked with, is
amazingly lifelike. Because they are much more dedicated to
their loves and hates, they seem more positive than real

people. But whereas a real person goes through many ups and downs and crises in the course of life, each fictional character is limited to the one crisis featured in the story, in which they play the central role.

You will see now how important it is to start each story in the right place. The characters who appear in your narrative only become interesting to the reader when it is obvious that some sort of crisis is brewing. The reader does not want any of the following offered for his inspection at the start of a story:

1. A potted biography of the 'I was born in' type which fills in background details about where the heroine went to school, what qualifications she had when she applied for her first job and how many jobs she did in the years afterwards until she married; when and where her children were born (by now reaching to fill in the background details on her husband as well) etc, etc.

Many beginner writers feel obliged to mention all this quite unnecessary detail, and they generally put it all into the opening paragraphs. It probably springs from our social upbringing which relies heavily on paperwork and references – the writer feels obliged to prove the credibility of his cast and act as a sort of guarantor for them. But as we have already seen, the reader will not be impressed – the scam will fail – so you know what to do with those opening pages filled with carefully worked-out detail. Keep looking until you find your real opening sentence – it might be near the bottom of page five.

2. Strict chronological order, another thing which constrains many beginners and can ruin their stories. Normally, the crisis in the lives of their characters will take place within only a few hours or days, and in such cases, their story must start as those few hours or days begin. Anything that the reader needs to know about earlier events or past history can be mentioned in passing as a random thought, a recollection or even a characteristic your heroine is aware of within herself which she is determined to overcome.

Begin your story when the crisis – whatever sort it is, and even if the characters are not aware that there is going to be one – is looming. Do not worry if you have to slip back a few times into the past with flash-backs to clear up a few points. For the vital hours or days during which your story takes place (even if it is only a subtle crisis, a shift in relationships or something of that sort) there should be a sense of charged living, that each moment is ticking by amid heightened feelings and emotions.

What takes place during a few highly charged hours can often make more impression on a person's life and memory than the events of the next twenty years, and this is the sort of significance your story should have. Short stories must never be written about people or events which are ordinary and unremarkable. All characters in fiction are, for the space when the story of their crisis is being narrated, larger than life, and occasionally of heroic dimensions.

3. Do not become tempted to give the readers a complete psychological dossier on your characters in order that their actions and motives can be understood. The story should start with a man or woman actively engaged in living, suddenly confronted – or about to be confronted – by a problem or conflict which will engage him until the story is finished. We have already seen that we do not need to know much about a character to become interested in him. Indeed, a story can still hold us fascinated if we have no idea at all of what is going on, or who the people involved are.

It is quite possible – and often adds to the power of a story – for a writer to keep his readers in the dark about his characters and their situation for practically the whole of the narrative. Explanations can often be not only irrelevant but positively off-putting. What holds the reader is not the amount of careful explanation he is given, but the fascination of actually being present as events progress and develop. In effect, your readers are holding their breath along with the characters, waiting for the outcome.

In general, try to avoid explaining anything in your stories. Your characters' actions and what they say will speak for them, they should not need an interpreter. There is one golden rule when you are writing fiction: show, not tell. Let the reader be right there in the middle of the action, making up his own mind about what is going on from the evidence before his eyes and that which is passing into his ears. The very last thing he needs – and if you try to do it, you are killing your story stone dead – is a commentary from yourself, pointing out every little detail, just in case he misses anything. Leave it to your characters and keep out of the way as much as possible.

The characters should, as we have just heard, be actively engaged in living when a story begins. This thought can assist you in identifying your gripping, reader-grabbing opening sentence. Do not start on a down, non-existent or relatively unimportant thought or statement like 'The sky was very blue that day' or 'I feel a bit depressed this morning,' Linda told Albert. 'I think I must be catching a cold or something.'

Catch your characters, as it were, in mid-action, and take the reader straight into the situation which is building up to the looming crisis. A shock opening will have your readers sitting up in their chairs. Something like:

The mirror had crashed down from the wall and broken. Fragments of glass lay everywhere, like frost. She thought: 'Seven years' bad luck!'

Another tip is to introduce your characters – your main character especially, who should be the first to appear – not formally, by their names, but as I have done above. 'She thought' gives the readers the impression they know this woman well, so well that they do not have to be told she is called Melanie and that she is anticipating some dire happenings in the near future. Her anticipation of dire happenings is implicit in that opening paragraph. The scene is set for the crisis, hints have been dropped that even the mirror breaking is a statement on the seriousness of the situation.

Get the readers involved right from the word go, do not waste time or words. See the story off to a good start.

SUMMARY

1. Do not begin a short story with the central character's birth and proceed to detail his life. Not in the final version, at any rate, though you may need to do this in early drafts.

2. Get your story completed in however tentative a form before you come back and work on it giving it a good beginning.

3. Many beginners need to 'write themselves into a story' and will include a great deal of material that can be cut later. Often the beginning you have given your story may be merely the springboard you needed to get started. Make sure you find where the real opening sentence is, and scrap the rest.

4. The action of any short story is concerned with some sort of turning point or crisis, whether this is a major upheaval or a subtle shift in relationships. The action has to work up to the resolution of the crisis and also to the artistic climax of the story itself.

5. The beginning of a story occurs when the moment of crisis is at hand. Your characters have lived only for this particular sequence of events in which they play the central role. Before and after, they are relatively anonymous, and readers will not want to hear about their past or future.

6. Do not give potted biographies in a short story. Even if the writer has to know every detail about his characters, readers do not want to hear them.

7. Do not keep to a strict chronological order if it would be more effective to tell your story in flashback or in some other way which involves moving around in time. But remember that the events of the story, the crisis or turning point will probably occur during only a few days, possibly a few hours. These are the important hours on which you need to concen-

trate, and there should be a feeling of charged living, heightened feelings and emotions.

8. No short story can ever be about people or events which are utterly ordinary and unremarkable. If they were, there would be no story.

9. Do not give detailed psychological dossiers on your hero and heroine. Readers can find them fascinating even if they know relatively little about them or how they think or feel. Try not to give explanations about anything in a short story.

10. In fact: show, not tell. Do not give commentaries.

11. Start the story when your characters are actively involved in living. Do not start on negative, downbeat, irrelevant or otherwise off-putting notes. A shock beginning can sometimes prove effective.

12. Do not be formal when introducing your characters to the reader. Let the reader feel they know each other, or if this is not possible, as though it is going to be easy to get to know each other. Let the reader feel involved right from the first word.

10
CHARACTER
AND PLOT

It might seem like a chicken and egg situation when you consider your story. Which should come first, the characters or the plot? The answer is that the characters are by far the most important. Without characters, there will be no story, for there will be nobody for the readers to identify with, nothing to touch their hearts and involve them emotionally. A story should never be written to appeal to the reader's logic or mathematical brain. The nearest you can get to this is a tightly-plotted crime story where the characters are, of necessity, secondary to the puzzle which has to be solved. But on the whole, you are catering for the feelings, the emotions, the dreams and aspirations, the hopes and longings of your readers. If they want large doses of logic and precision, they should take up crossword puzzles rather than read short stories.

On the other hand, however, your characters might well be intensely real and convincing, but if nothing happens to them, and they just sit about – in other words, if you have no plot to your story – the effect will be the same as if beautifully dressed marionettes lolled lifelessly in a box and never emerged to put on their show. So the plot too is very necessary.

What many people do not realise is that plot and characters are intertwined, they spring from each other. Because your characters are the people they are, they behave in the manner they do, and the incidents of your story take place. And in the same way, because your characters are the people they are, they will react in the manner they do to those incidents. You cannot force a plot on to your characters as though you were pulling a glove on to your hand. You have to allow them to lead you, in their own way, into the plot.

Your characters know far more, intuitively, about themselves than you do even though you are their author.

It was customary in the past to lay much more stress on plot. A plot was regarded (and sometimes, alas, still is) as a solid unit, a framework that would ensure the story would be solid and would not fall down. There were rules which aspiring story writers were encouraged to study, so that with little or no effort on their part, they could arm themselves with a cast iron plot round which to build their story.

One of the most dismaying things about plots is when you think up a really good one, and then discover it has already been used by someone else. If this has happened to you, I am afraid you are going to have to prepare yourself for rather a shock, since as we have already mentioned, it is a fact that every single plot has already been thought of.

You will never dream up a completely original plot – indeed, according to some authorities, there are only seven possible plots altogether. But this does not mean your stories will not be any good. For it is not the plot itself that matters, it is the treatment you – or any other writer – give to it which makes it interesting and fresh and readable.

Remember that (as Cecil Hunt reminds us) 'The octave has only eight notes but many an abiding melody can be contrived from them.' Mozart and Chopin and Beethoven could well have given up in disgust when they realised that there were only eight notes in an octave – a composer needs scope, freedom to spread himself out, they might have said. What can I possibly do with only eight notes? In the same way, a writer can add nuance, subtlety and the stamp of his own mind and that Writer's Eye which sees the world so individually, to a situation or plot that has appeared in some form hundreds of times before. And the reader will be fascinated and drawn effortlessly into the scam.

We have already come across some of the basic conflicts that can help make up a plot, and in order to stimulate the imagination, we will next examine a unique list of the 36 plots which, according to their compiler, cover every possible dramatic situation that can ever arise. The compiler is variously named as someone called Georges Polti, or as Count

Carlo Gozzi – and it is interesting to note that the list was approved and agreed with by both Goethe and Schiller.

Here are the great 36:

1. Supplication.
2. Deliverance.
3. Crime pursued by vengeance.
4. Vengeance taken for kindred upon kindred.
5. Pursuit.
6. Disaster.
7. Falling prey to cruelty or misfortune.
8. Revolt.
9. Daring enterprise.
10. Abduction.
11. The enigma.
12. Obtaining.
13. Enmity of kinsmen.
14. Rivalry of kinsmen.
15. Murderous adultery.
16. Madness.
17. Fatal imprudence.
18. Involuntary crimes of love.
19. Slaying of a kinsman unrecognised.
20. Self-sacrifice for an ideal.
21. Self-sacrifice for kindred.
22. Sacrifice for passion.
23. Necessary sacrifice of loved ones.
24. Rivalry of superior and inferior.
25. Adultery.
26. Crimes of love.
27. Discovery of a beloved one's dishonour.
28. Obstacles to love.
29. An enemy loved.
30. Ambition.
31. Conflict with a god.
32. Mistaken jealousy.
33. Mistaken judgement.
34. Remorse.

35. Recovery of a lost one.
36. Loss of beloved ones.

I have included this list to prompt your imagination rather than for you to consult it solemnly whenever you need a plot. Beware of becoming too reliant on this, or anything else which promises to take away the necessity to make your own decisions and use your own judgement. All new writers are reluctant to let go of any hand which seems as though it will guide them safely through the morass of indecision to literary stability – but it is this very independence of thought, the fact that you choose for yourself the way you will go, which will make your work mature and good.

So read the list – and then forget about it. Your plots (however hackneyed or however individual they might be) will arise from your characters, and your characters will spring from within yourself. So let us consider these characters in a little more detail.

Anyone can put together a description of a character including colour of hair and eyes, height, distinguishing marks and so on. The skill of a really good story writer is not to describe his characters but to bring them to life. Physical details and habits do not matter at all when compared to that vital spark of life which will convince the reader that these are real people.

And how does one achieve that vital spark? Again, the answer lies in the subconscious. Characters who seem perfect can often refuse to develop from a cardboard cut-out, while people you were not really interested in might suddenly begin to nag at your consciousness, always there, urging you to tell their story.

When you have your characters, you almost always have your plot. Most expert writers agree on this. 'When the characters are really alive before their author, the latter does nothing but follow them in their action, in their words, in the situations which they suggest to him,' said Pirandello, while Isaac Bashevis Singer declared: 'The characters have their own lives and their own logic, and you have to act accordingly.'

There are, however, some dissenting voices. Vladimir Nabokov is implacable that 'That trite little whimsy about characters getting out of hand; it is as old as the quills. My characters are galley slaves'. John Cheever, too, feels that 'The idea of authors running round helplessly behind their cretinous inventions is contemptible'.

What they are decrying is the concept of the author somehow standing dithering on the sidelines while his characters dash madly round doing exactly as they like. Such a picture would indeed make the author seem a fool, someone who had no control over what he was doing and no skill so that he had to let the affair muddle through on its own because he was unable to cope. Do not think of your characters in this way – rather imagine them as spirited animals who are 'trained, but never tamed' in the words of those who perform with wild beasts. When they come to life for you, your characters will be unpredictable, they will go through their paces as you and the story require them to, but there will always be that independence of spirit, that part of them which is beyond your control. If you ever do manage to subdue your characters to the extent that they perform passively, they might as well be dead, for you will have killed them. We can take it that even Nabokov's galley slaves were seething with rebellious fury as he cracked his whip across their shoulders while they bent to their task.

There are some simple methods to follow if you find it difficult to summon up memorable characters. As we have heard, colour of eyes and hair, or even detailed description of dress, can leave the reader cold. What matters – what will bring a character to life – is to know that person intimately, better than you know your husband or wife, to know them so that they are as familiar to you as the lines on your own hand, and that all details of their past, present – probably even future – existence are within your grasp. Such a feel for your characters goes far beyond the 'green eyes and chestnut hair' type of description.

In order to bring about this detailed knowledge, it is sometimes recommended that the writer compiles a detailed description of each character, including their previous history, likes and dislikes, idiosyncrasies, strengths and weaknesses, habits, ambitions, hopes and aspirations, loves and hates, etc. One person who swears by this method even advocates 'being' that character for a day and taking on the role as an actor would when preparing for a part – walking, talking and behaving as that character would, noting the result.

The one disadvantage with this method of character creation is that you can get so wrapped up in it that it becomes an end in itself, and in the enjoyment of what you are doing, you lose sight of the story. Never forget that always, it is your story which is your real aim.

Characters may sometimes be suggested by people you know, or even strangers who spark off a response in you. It is very rare that a real person can be lifted from life into the pages of fiction, even though all fictional characters have to seem utterly real. A real person, however interesting, would be much too complicated and many sided to fit easily into a narrative, but the relevant parts of him, the unusual habits, odd quirks or amusing little ways, might be exactly what will make your character.

Aldous Huxley sums this process up with great clarity: 'Of course I base my characters partly on the people I know – one can't escape it – but fictional characters are oversimplified; they're much less complex than the people one knows.'

Out of all the people you have ever met in your life, all the people you have ever seen casually, the films and books you have seen and read, the pictures you have viewed, from somewhere out of this great melting pot will come each character you create. They will be made up of bits and pieces – one person's eyes, another's lovely swan-like neck, another's voice. Of course, in the long run, each character is yourself, or some aspect of yourself, but transmuted by means of interweaving the images you have collected during your life into a creation that is uniquely itself.

It is very important that you do not fall into a trap that yawns for unsuspecting new writers, and use your stories to play out your own personal fantasies or wish-fulfilments. I went through this phase when I was in my teens and had begun to write passionate love stories with incredibly gorgeous heroes who appeared from nowhere and pressed bunches of mimosa or red roses into the hands of a heroine who was remarkably like myself. (It seems that I was also anticipating the romance of a certain tv commercial here, too. They also play on our personal fantasies in order to persuade us of the magic properties of the products they are promoting.)

Try to be aware of this aspect of your characters, and if you find – being honest with yourself – that one of them is a thinly veiled version of yourself, either fulfilling a personal fantasy or atoning for a past error, confessing a long-hidden guilt or simply recording some deeply felt episode in your past, sit back and take a long hard look at your work. Using your stories for your own ends is not good enough. You need to pass beyond that stage to where your characters are people in their own right, working out their own destinies. But it is a stage most beginners do pass through, so do not be dismayed to find that this particular milestone is the one you have just reached on your way to becoming a good writer. Carry on working, and you will progress and become more skilful.

THE 'STORY CONTENT' SCALE

The more familiar the writer is with his characters, the more real they are to the reader, the more subtle the actual plot of the short story may be. Indeed, if you examine the large numbers of short stories in existence, you will find, sooner rather than later, that quite often, there does not seem to be an actual storyline at all.

In some stories – the crime or puzzle stories that have already been mentioned – the plot and working out of the framework is all important. These we might well describe on a scale from 1 to 10 of 'Story Content' as of strength 9 or even strength 10. Character in such cases would have to be sketchy, almost cardboardy, just enough to fill in the gaps between the solid bars of plot.

Then there are other stories where the characters and the

incidents of the plot seem to be of about equal importance. Often such stories may lean heavily towards a twist ending that rounds the situation off for the characters. We might rate these as about strength 6 or 7 on the Story Content Scale.

When we get to the lower realms, where the Story Content falls as low as strength 4, or even strength 2, it seems as though we are not dealing with short stories as such at all. Where is the storyline? Where is the plot? Nothing happens, there might even appear to be no conflict, no interaction between the characters.

In fact, what is happening is that the story is assuming a form that is almost a type of shorthand. Some authorities compare this treatment of a short story to that of a poem – and indeed, often a very subtle strength 2 story, say, might well possess the intensity and discipline of a poem. There is far more common ground between a short story and a poem than there is between a short story and a novel.

Let us hear what a writer called C. Henry Warren (a contemporary of Cecil Hunt so far as I can discover) had to say in his book *The Writer's Art* about stories which we can consider very low on the Story Content scale. His words apply as vitally today as they did when he wrote his book:

'It is sometimes complained against the modern short story, by those unsympathetical to its more lyrical aspects, that it is more of a sketch than a story... But the aim of the short story writer need not necessarily be to tell a story, however briefly, in all its detail. If he has art enough, he can so portray a moment in life, a pose, a gesture, that it evokes the reader's imagination and compels *him* to complete the story, or enlarge it, according to his own fancy. Such a story or sketch, is like a pebble dropped into the still waters of a pond: where the stone falls, the quiet surface is broken into rings of tiny waves which widen until, infinitely small, they reach the limits of the shore. That is what a skilful sketch can do; by its impact with the reader's own mind it can set the ripples of imagination expanding until they are finally lost on far away shores.'

The Story Content Scale helps us to make sense of the fact that some stories are heavily reliant on their narrative content, while others merely sketch the events of the plot, and leave the reader to fill in the rest for himself. There is no rule that says either of these types of story is better than the other – they are different, that is all. However, it has to be said that the stories low on our scale, the sort where nothing much seems to happen and a great deal is left to the reader's imagination, are generally very much more difficult to write than the sort where the plot is clear and one can follow it through from beginning to end.

Unfortunately, a great many new writers prefer the idea of writing stories of 'literary merit' where the plot is practically non-existent, to doing a bit of hard work and putting some effort into their narrative. Needless to say, beginners seldom, if ever, succeed in writing lyrical, subtle sketches which are capable of turning into praiseworthy short stories. If you are thinking along these lines, do not waste your time. New writers progress down the Story Content scale rather than up it – aim first for a tight, well written story of strength 9 or 10, with a plot that complements your characters and gives the story a shape.

Later, when you have a great deal more experience, you can attempt lyrical, poetic efforts where the reader fills in the gaps and does most of the work. By which time you will have realised that in fact, writing stories where there is subtlety and poetic intensity requires just as much hard labour as writing a formula type of story with a clear-cut plot.

The conflict in a story generally portrays the central character or characters tying to make his or their way through opposing odds. The opposition may be of many and various different sorts – how to win the person he or she loves; how to persuade a figure of authority like a boss, government official or what-have-you to change their mind; how to overcome fear, tackle flying, driving or riding again after a bad accident; how to solve a crime, deal with a problem. You can write your story about anything so long as there is something for your main character to overcome – or sometimes, not overcome. In this case, the resolution of the problem would be in his or her final acceptance that things cannot be changed.

The central character in your story – and as we shall see, a short story needs to be written around one central character in the main – must be active rather than passive. And I am afraid it will not work if he or she achieves their aim by chance, accident or something which just happens so that things go right.

I have read many stories by beginner writers which deal with the problem of fear. This provides a good, strong emotion for a story – the central character is menaced, terribly afraid, but refuses to give in, fights on, and at the end, is saved, rescued or whatever. The trouble is, though, that often the writers have let the fear spring from being alone in a foreign city, lost in a strange place, thinking one is being followed in the dark of a lonely wood.

The ending in all such cases comes when the main character, after trying not to give way, sees a person he or she recognises, sees a familiar landmark, reaches the end of the wood and the lights which reveal there are no pursuers. All these stories fail because, as you can see, the solution to the problem does not come from the actions of the character but from chance, happenstance, the fact that 'there had been nobody there at all, it was just imagination.'

Even if a story deals with fear – or any similar emotion – which is 'all in the mind', the main character still has to do something, take some action to combat that fear. From the action taken, whether it has any relevance to the source of the fear or not, should come the resolution of the story's conflict.

Another sort of solution to problems which does not work is if the main character's troubles are solved not by his or her own actions, but by the actions of somebody else – a parent-in-law giving him or her a job, for instance. Other people can of course appear in your story – though not too many, remember you are restricted by the short story form and cannot have a huge cast as you could had you been writing a novel – but other people should not play major roles in the action, and should certainly not take the initiative. Focus should always be on your central figure, and he must struggle against whatever malignant influences seem to be gathered against him to achieve his own salvation, rather than have it provided for him. Even if he is doomed to fail, it should be a failure on his own merits, as it were, rather than a kick in the teeth from somebody who happened to have more money or more power.

We have seen how the characters and plot are intertwined, and how the plot springs from the type of people your characters are. Your characters must be actively involved in the plot, and will, in a cause and effect process, prompt developments to take place as a result of their efforts to sort out their difficulties. To these developments, they will need to react even further, and the plot becomes more and more involved. If outside happenings are imposed on your characters, and they simply accept everything without showing any sign of reaction or concern, neither they nor the plot will succeed in convincing your readers that the story bears any resemblance to real life.

The characters must play up to each other and toss the ball of the plot between them, and if they simply plod on, in a blinkered manner, while things happen around them which do not seem to have any significance to them, the whole point of the characters and plot are lost. They must interact with each other, so that in the end the conflict of interests works itself out satisfactorily. A plot can resemble a game of chess as the characters move in turn, now advancing, now retreating, but with much more emotional involvement than chessmen ever possess. One character takes some action or introduces a new element – another character reacts and makes his or her own move. And so on.

This sort of give and take is what makes a plot different to a simple sequence of events. In a sequence of events, anything can happen and each event bears no relation to the one that preceded it, or the one that will come after. In a plot, every action is a result of something someone else has said or done, or something that character has worked out for himself or herself, bearing their circumstances in mind. And what he or she decides to do about it will affect what the other characters in their turn are going to do next.

The fact that real people are neither all good or all bad, neither saints or sinners, but a mixture of both, can be immensely useful in assisting you to create believable characters. The fact that they have faults and failings, the fact that they might have weaknesses which prevent them from achieving all they hope to achieve, the fact that they are vulnerable and can be hurt – all of these will not only help you to work out credible plots for these characters whom you will come to love and feel chivalrous and protective about, but will actually bring them to life for you.

BY ANY OTHER NAME

Now for some practical advice. You will naturally want to give names to your characters, but it is very important that each character should have the right name. This may sound ridiculous, but it is not in fact so. Your characters have a right name each, and if you try to impose some other name on them, you could well spoil your whole story.

Often, their name will be the first thing that attracts you to a character. But in other cases, the name will not seem to come, and you are biting your lip wondering what on earth this exasperating woman is called. Do not dismiss such predicaments as ridiculous and fanciful. Wait until you get the name you know instinctively is right.

The name is more than just something to call your character, it *is* that character. And with your conscious mind, you will be able to tell your readers a great deal about each person from their name. First impressions, as with meeting strangers, count for a great deal. Is your heroine young and budding into womanhood, with a plainness that is going to flower into a startlingly unusual and piquant loveliness? Her name might come to you at once – one the reader will feel sums up the sort of character you have in mind. Jassy short for Jasmin, perhaps, if she is fair, or Zelda if she is bewitchingly dark. You would only be doing your story harm if you decided, against all your better judgement, to call her Myrtle or Gertie.

In the same way, you can indicate that a character whose name is Albert Groper is not one readers should take seriously; and that Ludovic X. Grubb is *not* going to be the hero. Names can indicate to the reader what sort of person they can expect that character to be, in the same way as the person's appearance would do if they had met face to face. But avoid too much verbal stereotyping – the right names, as I have said, will come to you.

Be aware that there are fashions in names, and that the class, social background, age and something of each person's character can be revealed in the names you give them. For instance, between the First and Second World Wars, some of the female names which were popular were flower ones – Rose, Violet, Daisy, Lily. These, together with others such as Edith and Doris, belonged to the 'lower classes', and the chances are that a woman called Daisy would now be in her sixties perhaps, have come from an impoverished background, probably had little formal education – though she might well possess the shrewdness of the 'working class' woman and have a good head for business – but still retain an innate sense of her place.

Nicknames too can tell the reader a great deal about a character. Does Daisy insist on being called by her full name, Daisy? Or does everyone call her Daise? Or has she at some stage decided to spell her name Dessi or Daizy? All these conjure up different aspects of her personality.

It is worth remembering that on the whole, the 'upper classes' keep to traditional names like Mary, Ann, Elizabeth, Caroline, Emma, though they do occasionally spring a surprise, but it is the 'lower classes' who seize on the names of popular singers, actresses and so on. Your male characters too will be affected by this same phenomenon – so do some investigation into names and their backgrounds so that you will be only too sympathetic when Charles Lancelot Fortescue insists to you that he must be known as Chaz or else he will not on any account appear in your story!

SUMMARY

A summing up of the points that have been mentioned concerning character and plot:

1. Character is of the greatest importance when writing a short story. Without characters with whom the readers can identify, there can be no story. The appeal of a short story is to the emotions rather than the intellect. But the characters must move and act, they must be involved in some sort of struggle or conflict or the story will be ruined.

2. Plot and characters are intertwined and spring from each other. The characters will reveal which ways they want the action of the plot to go. Trust your intuition so far as your characters are concerned, they know themselves better than you do.

3. All possible plots have been used at some time or another, and there are only a limited number of situations which can form the basis for a plot. But it is the treatment each writer gives his plot which makes it fresh and interesting.

4. Formal lists of possible plots should only be used to stimulate your imagination, not as cast iron foundations on which to work.

5. What matters about characters is that they should seem real and alive to the reader. Description and detail alone may not achieve this, they need to take on independence from their author and come to life in their own way.

6. A writer needs to know his characters intimately, and it is sometimes helpful to compile a dossier on each, filling in every detail of their past history and personal idiosyncrasies. If you wish, you can even act out the part of that particular character and note what sort of reaction he or she would get from those around them.

7. No real person can be lifted in his entirety into a story, but

details, habits, bits and pieces of many of the people you have known or met, seen or read of, will come together in your mind to form completely new, original characters who are your own creation and who will seem completely true to life.

8. Do not use the short story form to recreate episodes from your past that you want to celebrate or externalise, or to act out your own particular fantasies. If you find you are doing this, be aware that it is a phase through which inexperienced writers pass, and keep on working so that you progress to the next stage.

9. The narrative content of stories can be measured by the Story Content scale. This helps us to see that all short stories are fulfilling the same aims and following the same rules even though they might appear very different. In some, the plot is spelled out for the reader – in others, the plot is simply hinted at, and poetic, lyrical or other intensified qualities are stirred to life in the reader's mind so that he provides a good deal of the detail of the story himself.

10. Do not assume that the more arty sort of stories are easier to write – they are not. In fact they require far more skill than a straightforward story where there is a clear plotline.

11. The conflict which makes up a story plot can be of any sort, physical or mental, so long as it is between the central character and something outside himself – other people/natural forces/fate or even something such as fear, within himself. The story starts where the moment of crisis is at hand, it builds up in intensity through one, perhaps two lesser climaxes (depending on how long the story is) to the final climax and resolution of the conflict/struggle at the end. The reader has to feel satisfied at the outcome, and that the ending was right for the story, even if it is not what he had hoped for. A twist ending is not always necessary and often might seem too contrived. Let integrity and your own sense of truth and rightness dictate your endings rather than a sense of slickness or commercialism.

12. The central character must always be active rather than passive. He must take action, not just wait for things to sort themselves out, or turn to others for the answer to his problem. Even if he fails, it must be because of his own actions, not because he was pushed out of the way by somebody bigger or stronger. He must always retain the initiative in your story, even if this only allows him to fume and wish he could say or do what he wanted to, instead of being inhibited by some inside or outside influence.

13. The difference between a sequence of events and a plot is that a sequence of events is unrelated, while in a plot, each happening is linked to what went before and what will come after. Characters inter-react and the actions of the plot grow into a linked, tightly formed chain that binds them together. There has to be a sense of inevitability in a plot, a feeling that 'of course, it could not have happened any other way, not considering the sort of people they were'.

14. Characters should be neither saints nor sinners, neither all good nor all bad. They have weaknesses as well as strengths, they have vulnerable points as well as their own particular form of aggression. By and large, however, they must act consistently throughout the story, and not do anything utterly out of character or unexpected unless there is a good reason for it. Usually, the reasons for this sort of behaviour are: they are insane; they are under terrible pressure and stress and are about to have a breakdown or otherwise go insane; they are mad with jealousy.

15. Make sure your characters have the right names that suit them and feel comfortable for you as the author. Do not try to impose names that do not fit. And be aware of the social history and trends which are reflected in names and which you can use to assist you in making your characters interesting and believable.

11
CONSTRUCTION AND VIEWPOINT

It is all very well to talk about short stories containing struggle and conflict, to emphasise that plot arises from the actions of the characters, and to mention that the story must begin when the moment of crisis is at hand rather than too early or too late. But still new writers may not find it clear as to exactly how a short story is constructed. So we will now consider the actual physical rules of construction, rather than the emotional, spiritual or other content which arises from the subject of the story itself.

Much of the construction will depend on the length of the story. All we have established so far in this direction is that a short story is a work of prose fiction of variable length, and that the length will depend on the editor and market for which the story is being written. But at the start of your writing career, especially when you are still finding your feet and practising your story writing, you need not bother too much about length unless you are actually writing with a certain market in mind. Let each story find its own length.

And believe me, it will. Just as there is a right place to start, there is also a right place where the story will reach its natural climax and ending.

The story must start off, as we have seen, with some sort of indication that something is, if not about to happen, then potentially worthy of our interest. The tension must be set up right at the start, so that the reader is gripped. From then on, the story proceeds in a series of small climaxes or confrontations between the various elements which make it up, with lesser periods of relative calm in between when the tension is allowed to relax a little.

In a story of two or three thousand words, there might –

depending on whether the pace of the story is fast or slow – be room for two, perhaps three main climaxes in all, including the final big climax and resolution at the end. There might in any story be lesser climaxes, little crossings of swords between the characters, which can punctuate the narrative, but the nature of a short story restricts the writer in a way which does not affect the writer of novels. Do not try to cram too much into a relatively small number of words, and do not try to include too much confrontation and climax. There has to be a sort of rhythm in the intensifying and lessening of conflict and tension in order to hold the interest of the reader, but too much, too quickly or even too slowly will mean that the story is badly constructed and it will not work.

In order to unify a short story, and in order for the reader to feel involved right from the start, it is customary for the story to be told from the viewpoint of one main character who plays the central role. He or she may tell the story in their own words, speaking in the first person as 'I', or the story may be told in the third person, in the words of the author, who will refer to the central character, along with the others, as 'he' or 'she'.

But the story is generally told from the point of view of the central character, and though the reader is aware of what he or she is thinking, no attempt is made at an omnipotent knowledge of what other people think, what they feel, what they are going to do next. Along with the central character, the reader waits breathlessly and tries to guess what is going on in the minds of the rest.

Sometimes, the central character is not the one who tells the story. In this case, the narrator is called the 'viewpoint' character, and he provides a commentary on affairs from a relatively humble position in the story. All kinds of individuals have been used as viewpoint characters. One story I read told of the passionate romance which developed between a young woman and the man she fell in love with. In this case, the central character was the young woman, but the viewpoint character who told the story was her Siamese cat!

Onlookers can make useful viewpoint characters. In the cases of Sherlock Holmes and Hercule Poirot, for instance, the great detectives themselves are not entirely likeable people with their arrogance and obsession with trivia. If they were to narrate their cases themselves, they would also sound unpleasantly smug and complacent, since they invariably know the answer to everything. The idea of having a rather dumb sidekick who is amazed at the recurring genius of his talented friend solves a lot of problems.

Everything, every word and sentence of dialogue, every adjective or other piece of description, everything must pull its weight and be there for a purpose. You might not get this right in the first draft, but careful editing and honing down when you have finished the story should ensure that there is no superfluous word, comma or even space which is being carried unnecessarily.

This applies also to characters and sub-plots. Few, if any, successful writers of short stories have written tales of under 5,000 words, say, involving 50 characters, unless 48 of those were a mob threatening the other two. The more characters you include, the less chance you will have to develop them as real people, and the more cardboardy they will have to be. A wonderful example to study is Hemingway's story *Indian Camp*, where within about 2,000 words, a small boy (the central character and viewpoint character), his father and his Uncle George are made vitally alive with a mere handful of words. This is the work of a great master – aim for a similarly high standard, but do not become disillusioned if you do not achieve it, not yet, anyway.

Another brilliant example to study for construction, character, plot and all the elements we have been discussing is James Thurber's *The Secret Life of Walter Mitty*, which creates a complete world (universe, almost) within some 2–3,000 words.

It is worth noting that often, when you study a story by a great writer, you may find it difficult to spot the way in which it has actually been put together. You may feel there never was any careful development of tension and conflict, that the whole thing just fell into place and turned out to be right. But no story just happens. The apparent simplicity, the lack of strain or obviousness, the difficulty in being able to spot the seams where the cloth of the story was joined up illustrates the true skill and mastery which a great master of his craft has worked hard to achieve.

In case you do wonder where the tension and plot-lines are with Mr Walter Mitty, the conflicts run between himself and the status quo, himself and his wife, himself and his inability to change the situation which, while being hilarious to the reader, is almost unbearably poignant if considered seriously. The final climax comes with his appreciation that he is living in a fantasy world, and his establishing of his right to remain there, the only place where he can be truly happy.

In the same way as you must restrict your characters, you must also restrict any secondary or sub-plots. There is no room in a few thousand words for anything in the plot line except the central thread which involves your main character. If your story is mainly concerned with a woman's effort to break from her brutal husband – to grow up and establish herself as an individual for the first time in her life – then that should provide more than enough twists and turns, small climaxes and short breaks of tension, to take you through. Almost certainly, there will be no room for a secondary plot about her child's problems with dyslexia and what the teacher at Carley's school thinks should be done about it. Or even your heroine's efforts to win First Prize at the local Dog Show with Pooch, her rag-bag of a mongrel.

Keep your incidents, scenes, dialogues, sharp and to the point, try to see the thread of your story running clearly through it – any suggestion of vagueness or rambling will mean the reader loses interest straightaway.

It is sometimes suggested that a good story is constructed in much the same way as a piece of music or a ballet – that it is choreographed or orchestrated. Characters, plot, incidents and all the other ingredients are put together by the author in such a way that the effect is as aesthetically pleasing as *Swan Lake* or Bruch's *Violin Concerto*.

If you can achieve this sort of artistic rightness about your story as well as give your readers a good read, the chances are that you might well be one of those talented people we mentioned earlier on in the book – the creative geniuses of this world. But even if you are not, we can at least aim for the right impression, and bear in mind the various methods of orchestrating and choreographing our work as we write.

The shape of the story itself may have all the qualities of a beautiful vase, the lovely curves of form, the balance and symmetry. There is a story called *The Gift of the Magi* by O. Henry, which possesses this overall shape to it. It tells of a penniless young couple who wanted to give each other something wonderful for Christmas – but they could afford nothing. So, secretly, each undertook their own small plan; each sold the only thing of value they possessed in order to purchase their gifts. The man sold his watch to buy his wife combs for her hair: she had her lovely hair cut and sold it in order to buy a fob for his watch. You see the point I am making? How could there be a more poignant pas de deux in the whole of classical ballet, or a more lovely duet than this in the world of opera?

SUMMARY

1. The length of a story is largely governed by the requirements of the market for which it is being written. Otherwise, if it is being written purely for pleasure or as practise, it should find its own correct length.

2. The story must start with tension and a gripping of the reader, and then build up in a series of climaxes or confrontations between the characters, with moments of calm in between.

3. Two or three thousand words will allow for perhaps two or three main climaxes (though of course, this is not a hard and fast rule, and you can break it with no compunction if you feel you need to). These include the main climax and resolution which comes at the end.

4. Do not try to include too much, or have too few conflicts. If the story is badly constructed, top-heavy or too long drawn out, it will not work.

5. A short story is generally told from the point of view of the central, most important character. They may speak in their own words as 'I' or be referred to by the author as 'he' or 'she'. In the first case, the story is said to be written in the first person, while in the second, it is written in the third person.

6. Though the reader is aware of what the central character thinks and feels, he does not know what is going on in the minds and hearts of the others. Like that person, he has to try and guess.

7. The person who tells the story is referred to as a viewpoint character. Sometimes it is the central character, but in other cases, it may be someone else who might not play a large part in the story, and may be only an observer of the activities of the central character. A viewpoint character who observes can often be useful to solve problems of characterisation which might have proved difficult if the main character had told the story himself.

8. Do not include too many characters. If there are a lot, you will not be able to develop them so they seem real and they will be unconvincing.

9. Do not imagine that stories written by great writers just happened. Their apparent simplicity and ease of writing are tributes to the writer's mastery of his craft.

10. Do not try to include too many sub-plots. In most short stories, the main thread is all important. Every word must pull its weight, and you must aim for sharpness and clarity.

11. Aim to bring to your story a sense of shape, form, line, artistic rightness. Keep trying, even if you never quite get it right. This sort of aesthetic beauty is the hallmark of great talent, probably of genius – but we can at least have this as the standard we set ourselves, even if we fall short.

12
DIALOGUE

How important is dialogue? If you think of it as just the words the characters say, consider the script of a play for a moment. The story is made up entirely of dialogue and every single thing the author wants the audience to know about what his characters think, feel and actually *are* has to be put across in those vital words.

So the skilful creation of dialogue, and an ear for what people say, how they say it and – most of all – for what they do not say is very necessary for the writer of short stories. Even if you do not include large chunks of dialogue in your writing, every word your characters say has to fulfil several functions, not just fill up the space between the inverted commas.

Why is dialogue used in stories at all? There are some writers who never include any, some stories where nothing is said, and they do not seem to suffer from any lack because there is no dialogue. So what difference does it actually make? In the first place, a good deal about dialogue will depend on the individual writer. Some people prefer to write cerebral sorts of narratives where everything goes on in the characters' heads, or in memory or in set pieces where meaning glances are more often apparent than actual speech between the characters. If you feel no need at all to use dialogue, and your work seems to be going well in all other respects, consider what functions dialogue fulfils, decide whether you could better your work by learning how to use it, and if you think there is no need, then you can forget about it, as obviously it does not suit your own particular style.

If, however, (like most beginner writers) you are having difficulty in writing the dialogue you want to include between your characters, we will now investigate this problem.

109

First, why do we use dialogue and what is it there for? It is to tell of verbal communication between the characters, whether the communication is one of love like 'I love you' or one of hate like 'You pig, I hate you'. And the reason why direct speech is used (each character speaking their line within inverted commas) is so that the reader will feel he is actually hearing and seeing the scene play itself out before his eyes, he is actually there as the fateful words are said. Indirect speech, where the author reports what was said afterwards, does not have the same impact, the same sense of realism, as though we were there at the moment everything happened.

But if you start listening carefully to the things people say in the everyday world around you, and compare them with the sort of dialogue you find in short stories, you will begin to see that fictional dialogue bears almost no resemblance to the speech of real life. It gives the impression that it does, and readers will often praise a story because it was 'so real, the way they spoke to each other was so true to life.' All of this is part of the scam. Our first point is that fictional dialogue is completely artificial and plays an entirely different role to what we say to each other in reality.

In real life, people have 24 hours in every day to say what they want to say to those around them: in a short story, they may, if they are lucky, have a few hundred words. So it is necessary that fictional dialogue must be condensed to the tightest possible conciseness, that there must be no rambling, waffling, changing the subject, wandering from the point, suddenly remembering what they were 'going to tell you yesterday, only I forgot.' Everything in fictional dialogue must be relevant to the story, in one of the following two ways, or else it should be left out.

Dialogue performs two main functions. The first is that it furthers the plot. Each scene where the characters talk to each other must carry the plot forward – as, indeed, must scenes where there is silence. Everything in the story must carry the plot forward, it must continue to progress from the opening line and never become static or padded or stop moving. So scenes of dialogue can assist in climax planning, pulling the tension tighter, confrontations, declarations, all the things which will mark small milestones as the story progresses.

The second function of dialogue is to tell us something about the characters, and help to foster the illusion of their reality. We have already seen that fictional characters are less dimensional than people in real life, and they certainly have far less to preoccupy their minds, since they have only the main struggle/conflict/crisis with which the story is concerned to think about. They do not suddenly get involved with saving the flora and fauna of Greenland, or start wanting to do deep sea diving to find buried treasure, since it seems to be an easier way of getting rich than waiting to come up on the pools. They keep to their own story, their own crisis, and do not overlap (or should not) into other potential plots.

How can dialogue reveal character and help to convince the reader the characters are real when not only the characters, but the dialogue itself, is fake? You may well ask, but this is where the whole art and skill of writing comes in. The amateur who spins a tale down at the pub, or the mother who tells her child a story at bedtime, is quite unaware of this aspect of writing technique, and even if they were aware, they would not be able to cope with it. But we, in our capacity as confidence tricksters and workers of the scam, are going to learn how to cope so that we take dialogue in our stride.

Do not expect to grasp this technique overnight. The first thing you need to do is to start listening, as I have already mentioned, to what people are saying around you, every-where you go. Listen in to other people's conversations. An experienced writer does this automatically in the same way as he uses his Writer's Eye. I personally have become adept over the years at being able to hold a conversation with one person at the same time as I am eavesdropping on another conversation – sometimes, if it seems necessary, two others – and being able to cope with all this without any of the parties being aware that I am doing so. Another interesting writer's habit I have long since acquired is being able to read docu-ments or letters upside-down when they are on desks in front of me or in other people's hands.

When you start to listen to what sort of dialogue is going on all around you, you will quickly realise two things – that most of what people say is not what they mean, and that what they actually do want to communicate does not get put into words at all, and generally remains unsaid. It is when you start to put this sort of knowledge and awareness of how people speak (or do not speak) into your work that your dialogue will start to sound fresh and vivid as well as real.

Dialogue can be on many levels. There is the superficial level of 'Good morning' and 'How are you?', the trivial chit-chat which keeps the wheels of polite society smoothly rolling. There is the slightly deeper level of everyday conversation in a family, say, where problems about homework, a child's school sports, what the husband's or wife's day has been like, local gossip and news, will fill up most of the evening, together with comments on 'what's on the box' and plans for tomorrow or the weekend.

But as you descent further, the deepest levels of dialogue speak from the soul, from the stricken heart, the most vulnerable centres of our whole being. No wonder that people might admit cautiously that they love their family, or that they are rather afraid of thinking about dying, but are more often than not afraid to speak out on such matters. Englishmen, in particular, were renowned in fiction of the twenties and thirties for always keeping that stiff upper lip, for never letting go, for never letting an emotive word pass their lips. Many men still behave in that way today – listen and you will hear them sheer off a subject if it is going to start delving into the depths of what they think and feel.

Few lines of dialogue will contain this intensity of feeling. It will be far more realistic if the girl asks:

'Do you really love me? Truly?' and the man (who does love her) turns away, clears his throat, fiddles with his watchstrap, and then says diffidently: 'You know very well.'
'Yes, but say it.' Her hand was stealing along the back of his neck, ruffling the points of hair. Her voice shook.

'Say it. Tell me.'

'Well, all right, I do.' It was a half-shrug.

'Do what?' she pleaded, and he snapped out:

'Love you. There you are. Now come on, let's go, I'm getting cold.'

But let us say that, in response to the girl's plea, the hero had replied in silky tones:

'Darling, you know I love you. You're my world, you're the only thing that means anything to me in this whole boring and futile existence. I adore you – I worship you – to merely love you would be to deny you your rightful dues'.

Would this mean the hero loved the heroine more than the first man? No – but it would mean that (a) The story was a send-up poking fun at romance or, (b) The hero was a slimy creep who was only out for what he could get before he threw her over or, (c) The writer had not listened to what was going on around him and had no ear as yet for good dialogue.

Imagine yourself listening to a conversation between several people you know, in the dark, so that you cannot see who is speaking. Would you be able to tell who was talking at any particular moment? But of course, you would. Gran always gives that autocratic little cough before she starts to speak, and Dolly says: 'Yes, but have you considered all the alternatives, Mother?' in that strained voice, as though she is only keeping her temper with an effort. And the kids' voices would be light, high, exasperated.

'Gordon Bennet, Gran, it's only a powercut! It's not the ruddy Blitz.'

'Could be a Close Encounter though, d'you think? Maybe we'll see the UFO in a minute.'

It is what your characters say that will tell your readers what they are and who they are. Character is not, as we have seen, created by means of adverbs and descriptive words. The readers must hear and see the pattern of each different mind speaking through the words that are used and hear the character emerging, rather than have it superimposed upon the dialogue.

In addition, a great deal of dialogue is very devious, so that the characters are not only not saying what they mean, they are trying hard not to mean what they say. In a way, although dialogue represents communication between your characters, it is also the greatest barrier that stands between them and their understanding of each other. If they could communicate by means of ESP or telepathy, there would be far less misunderstanding between the characters (as there would between real people) and so fiction, which depends to a very large extent on deviousness and misunderstanding, would suffer as a result.

People use dialogue to protect themselves, to keep their secrets – however innocent those secrets may be. There is a classic tale of a man who went down a street knocking on every door. When the householder answered, the man said cryptically: 'Flee! All is discovered.' And there were some hasty flights from the street that night. For every one of us has a secret or secrets we want to keep to ourselves. Crime stories deal with real skeletons, but nearly every person – and certainly every fictional person – has some secret skeleton in the cupboard, some sin, guilt, shame or other lapse from grace, however trivial it might seem to other people, that we would die rather than reveal to the world.

Dialogue often reflects our efforts to protect our secrets, and sometimes we do this without even being aware of it. For instance, a girl who is smitten by a certain man will go red and become elaborately nonchalant and casual if his name is mentioned. This is, to others, a dead give-away, of course, but she is automatically putting up her protective barriers for fear of rejection. She would never dream – unless she was a very different sort of character – of saying: 'Yes, I think he's rather a pet. I've got my eye on him as a matter of fact, I think you're going to see him round here quite a bit in the next few months.'

Dialogue can assist enormously in helping to put your characters across as real people, but the point you must remember is that same one we keep coming across – that every word must count. In dialogue especially, you cannot afford ramblings round the subject, even if the character is a rambly sort of person. The effect can be created with very few words, if those words are carefully chosen and your whole sequence is tightly and carefully written. It might even read as though the characters arc taking all the time in the world and their conversation is going on for ever.

SUMMARY

1. Dialogue is one of the most vital skills a writer needs to learn. Take as your example the dialogue in a play, where every single thing the author wants the audience to know has to be put across by means of the spoken word.

2. Dialogue's task is to fulfil certain functions, not just fill up the space between the inverted commas.

3. Usage of dialogue depends on the individual writer. Some people do not use much dialogue, if any, but it does not spoil their work. If you feel no need for dialogue, do not feel constrained to use it, but do first consider whether it would benefit your work before you make your decision.

4. Dialogue exists to illustrate verbal communication between the characters. In direct speech (where the lines the characters say are set between inverted commas) the reader is made to feel that he is there, part of the scene, listening as the action takes place. Indirect speech lacks this impact.

5. Listen carefully to everything that is said around you. Try to cultivate an ear for dialogue.

6. Fictional dialogue bears little resemblance to the way people speak in real life, even though well written dialogue always sounds real. But fictional dialogue is completely artificial and is there for a purpose, while everyday dialogue is relatively pointless.

7. There is only a small space and a few words for you to put your dialogue across successfully, so whatever your characters have to say must be condensed and concise.

8. All dialogue must be relevant to the story, and must perform one of two functions – it must either further the plot or it must reveal character and help to foster the illusion that the characters are real.

9. People in real life rarely say what they mean, and will not generally say what they feel. It is on these real life characteristics that the fictional characters you create will base their own artificial dialogue, since what people say in real life is the raw material of fictional dialogue.

10. Dialogue can exist on many levels, from the superficial to the depths of emotional intensity. In real life (and therefore in fictional dialogue) characters rarely remain on an extremely intense level, and will often try to avoid the deepest levels altogether.

11. Your characters must be able to be identified by what they say and how they say it, rather than having external characteristics or descriptions imposed on them.

12. Though dialogue is a means of communication, it is also a barrier which people erect to protect themselves from hurt. Nearly everyone has a secret they do not want the world to know, and they will use what they say to keep that secret to themselves – often unaware that they might be giving it away in the process.

13. Every word of dialogue must count.

13
SCENE AND DESCRIPTION

The amount of description – both of the scene and of the characters, and action and so on – which should be included bothers many new writers. They think there is some sort of standard rule, and are afraid to include too little or too much.

In fact, as with most of the other technicalities of story writing, a lot will depend on you and on your story and only you can really tell exactly how much description you need. If there is a rule, it is – when in doubt, leave out. It is far better to describe sparsely and economically than to overload the reader with huge chunks of descriptive paragraphs. Remember that any time you are stopping to describe something, you are holding up the action. Description should be more in the nature of a quick prompt here and there, when the readers cannot be expected to know what something looks, or sounds, like. It is not a means to an end.

It is, of course, necessary for you to set the scene of your story. The action has to take place in some particular spot, and the characters must (unless this is science fiction) be tied in some way to their own particular part of the countryside, their own special house made of bricks and mortar, their own seat on the plane, their own hotel room when on holiday. But do not make the mistake of feeling that you have to describe the setting before you actually get on with the story itself. We have seen that we do not need to know a great deal about the characters before we can become interested in them. Equally, we do not need to know everything about the scene before we can proceed with the action.

Ideally, the scene should help to reveal the characters to us, rather than be told to us in a guide-book type of manner.

Consider these two openings:

> The farm nestled in a hollow in the hills. Lory's family
> had lived there for generations, and she never failed to
> think how fortunate she was in living in such a beautiful
> place – the green hills around, the sparkling streams, the
> birds that woke her each morning and the wild flowers
> that starred the fields when she walked the acres with a
> stick in her hand, Ben the dog beside her.

How does that rate when compared with this?

> Lory swung back the little casement window, set in two-
> feet thick walls which kept the farm cool even in the
> hottest weather.
> What a glorious day!
> Her face was alight as she called back to the black-
> bird on the lilac tree, and at the sound of her voice, old
> Ben came trotting – rather sedately now, even though he
> tried to pretend he was still just a puppy – round the
> side of the house.
> 'Hi, Dad,' Lory cried, seeing her father cross the
> corner of the yard. 'It's the first day of spring!'
> 'The College is opening, all the same,' her father
> grunted drily. 'And you'll need your Computer Studies
> my lass. Communing with nature never brought in
> anything like a good week's wage.'
> 'You're just an old pain, Dad,' Lory told him affec-
> tionately, but she turned to hurry into her uniform and
> run down to help get the breakfasts.

The best sort of description is of unusual or otherwise memorable details, which the reader will feel adds an extra dimension to the story. We have already seen that descriptions of
physical details do little to bring characters to life. Brown
hair, dark eyes, a slim figure, long legs – none of these really
adds anything to a piece of writing. But if you described your
heroine as possessing a wonderfully attractive and lovely
voice, for instance, this is something that stands out:

He could never describe afterwards what she looked like, but her voice, that low blend of syllables and phrases that made the English language sound like the most beautiful music he had ever heard, was, he knew, going to haunt him for ever.

The same applies to descriptions of scenes. Try to avoid full-frontal descriptions of houses, doors, windows, roof, chimneys. Again, keep to just one or two telling details – the fact that birds nested in the chimneys of the Great House and you could see them winging their way home against the sunset, for instance, will conjure up quite a detailed picture of the house itself as well as the grounds.

Always bear in mind that the most effective description is that which the readers provide themselves. There is a well known story of a small boy who, when asked whether he preferred to watch the plays on tv or listen to the plays on the radio, answered that he liked the radio plays best 'because the scenery is so much nicer'. Your readers have imaginations which they are ready and willing to put to good use to assist with all the right effects. Let them contribute to the success of your story. Do not force your own descriptions on them – allow them, with a gentle hint here and there, to do all the hard work in this direction themselves. And meanwhile, of course, you are free to keep the action going.

One of the most important points to bear in mind about description and scene-setting is that the writer needs to be selective. One or two careful descriptive phrases could well leave the reader with the impression that he has just read a detailed two-page description, and he will feel he knows everything about that particular subject. He will also feel that this writer is so enjoyable, because (as with the radio plays and the small boy) 'the scenery and the descriptions are so good'.

Keep your paragraphs short, in general. Very long paragraphs, particularly if these are filled with description, have a rather indigestible effect on the reader, so unless your story is going to be of a deeply dramatic, intense sort – which I do not advise beginners to attempt at this stage unless for amusement or experiment – you will be hindering your own efforts at keeping the reader's interest.

THE PROCESS OF DESCRIPTION

What happens with description and scene setting is a three-fold process. First, the writer visualises in his mind the scene or view or clothes the character is wearing or whatever. He must be quite clear about this, so that he could describe it all in great detail if he needed to. In fact, it may help when you are training yourself towards writing skill, if you actually do this. Put down all the description of your scene, your character, the moonlight on the lake, the country mansion, whatever.

Then move to the second stage of the process. Once the writer has visualised his mind-picture, he must transfer this to the mind of his reader, by means of the written word. But because fiction is an art form, and because the short story is very limited so far as wordage goes, it is not possible for the long and detailed descriptions the writer has noted down to be included. Therefore the description must be condensed to its minimum so that it will lose nothing in the telling, but will consist of a fraction of the writing space and reading time. Remember that in all aspects of fiction, there is no need to spell out every word. The reader, as we have just seen, will be more than willing to meet you halfway.

So in stage two, you go through your detailed description and ruthlessly cut out any bits that are not necessary because the reader will assume them anyway, or they are duplicating some other detail, or they just do not matter. Try to encapsulate the spirit and main outline of your description in just a few phrases. Yes, this is possible; and in fact professional writers do it all the time. But it is a skill that needs to be learned, so enjoy yourself learning it. As you progress, you will be amazed at how skilful you become at cutting out extraneous material.

The third stage is to transfer, by means of your carefully chosen phrases and details, the picture you had in your mind into the mind of your reader. There is one thing to be aware of here. What a writer sees in his mind when he thinks up his story, and what his reader sees in his mind when he reads that story, are entirely different. It is impossible to transfer the exact picture you see into the mind of anybody else. You might well describe a character who looks exactly like the Botticelli Venus, and go to great lengths to put this across. Your reader will get the picture all right, but what he sees might be a perfect likeness of Madonna or even Marilyn Monroe. Two minds cannot think alike, and you must learn not to be surprised when readers misunderstand what you were trying to say.

Every writer of short stories must know the scene in which his story is set as clearly as he knows his characters, even though he might not put 99 percent of the detail on paper. The authority we have already mentioned, with which the narrator grasps and holds the attention of his reader, has a great deal to do with how well the writer knows his background. But remember that as the story progresses, the reader will see it not through your eyes, but through the eyes of your characters, and they, like readers, will not see things the same way that you do.

If your character is happy, he will see the scene very differently than he would if he were badly depressed, worried or anxious. We see what we want to see, and even though the scene may be exactly the same, two people, if asked to describe it, would describe it in different ways, depending on their mood, their emotional state, their general attitude to living at that moment. Bear in mind always that your story is told, acted by and orchestrated by your characters. If possible, keep yourself out of the picture and let them do their own describing – a good deal of it can be done in what they say to each other, and what they think and feel.

Everything, every technical skill, works together if the author is experienced enough, to create an overall effect which will seem utterly natural.

As an example of brilliant use of description and scene setting, as well as dialogue and the other techniques we have already mentioned, here is the opening to Katherine Mansfield's story *Her First Ball*. Study this carefully, for it will teach you a great deal.

Exactly when the ball began Leila would have found it hard to say. Perhaps her first real partner was the cab. It did not matter that she shared the cab with the Sheridan girls and their brother. She sat back in her own little corner of it, and the bolster on which her hand rested felt like the sleeve of an unknown young man's suit; and away they bowled, past waltzing lamp-posts and houses and fences and trees.

'Have you really never been to a ball before, Leila? But, my child, how too weird – ' cried the Sheridan girls.

'Our nearest neighbour was fifteen miles,' said Leila softly, gently opening and shutting her fan.

Oh, dear, how hard it was to be indifferent like the others! She tried not to smile too much; she tried not to care. But every single thing was so new and exciting... Meg's tuberoses, Jose's long loop of amber, Laura's little dark head, pushing above her white fur like a flower through snow. She would remember for ever. It even gave her a pang to see her cousin Laurie throw away the wisps of tissue paper he pulled from the fastenings of his new gloves. She would like to have kept those wisps as a keepsake, as a remembrance. Laurie leaned forward and put his hand on Laura's knee.

'Look here, darling,' he said. 'The third and the ninth as usual. Twig?'

Oh, how marvellous to have a brother! In her excitement Leila felt that if there had been time, if it hadn't been impossible, she couldn't have helped crying because she was an only child and no brother had ever said 'Twig?' to her; no sister would ever say, as Meg said to Jose that moment, 'I've never known your hair go up more successfully than it has tonight'.

But, of course, there was no time. They were at the drill hall already; there were cabs in front of them and cabs behind. The road was bright on either side with moving fan-like lights, and on the pavement gay couples seemed to float through the air; little satin shoes chased each other like birds.

SUMMARY

1. There is no standard rule about how much or how little description should be included in a story. It should suit the story and feel right to the writer. If in any doubt leave it out, as it is better to have too little description rather than too much. Make sure there is enough to put a clear picture across without overloading the reader with unnecessary details.

2. Description and scene setting can delay the action. Try to incorporate the description into the action rather than tell it guidebook style.

3. Try to describe unusual or memorable details rather than ordinary and unspectacular points. The reader does not want to hear a boring description which might apply to anywhere or anything. He wants to know what makes these characters and this story special.

4. Readers provide a great deal of the description and scene setting with their own imaginations. Let them help you to make your story vivid and colourful. Encourage them to use their minds rather than forcing descriptions upon them.

5. Be very selective about your description. One or two carefully chosen phrases or details can give the reader the impression he has read a full description lasting several pages and knows everything. He will also feel you are a very good writer of descriptive prose.

6. Try to keep paragraphs containing description short.

7. Transferring the image from your mind to that of the reader is a three-fold process. First get the picture clear in your own mind, possibly even write a full description down. Secondly, cut out all unnecessary and extraneous material

until your description is as concise as you can make it. Thirdly, use careful selection and work your description in with the narrative in order for your reader to see what you want to show him. He will not see the same picture you do, but this will not matter.

8. Know your scenes and what you are describing very well, even if you only include a fraction of the description you might have used. This gives your work authority.

9. Your characters will view the scenes in your story differently according to their mood, state of mind and general outlook. Their reactions will vary in the same way that yours vary to the reader's. Try to let them do their own describing – include bits of description in their dialogue, for instance.

10. Try to weave all the strands of technique together so that the story flows smoothly and the different aspects of it are interwoven into a unified whole. Use one technique to bolster up another, and the other way round.

14
PACE, MOOD, ATMOSPHERE, SUSPENSE

There are various intangibles which help to give a story richness and quality, which we will deal with under this general heading. The first item we will discuss is pace.

Pace is the speed at which the story moves, the speed at which things happen. In a short story, this is very important because the success of the whole story might well depend on keeping the pace right. You need to be aware of what type of story yours is, whether it is a quick, snappy short short, a longer and more moody story of memory, say, nostalgia, emotion or feeling. Superficial narratives with sketchy characters are generally quicker moving than those where the characterisation is very detailed. As you can imagine, it is impossible to get a very detailed plot, very detailed characters and a lot of other detail all into one short story. There has to be an emphasis on one particular aspect of your technique.

The pace of a story means that events move quickly, or they move in a much more leisurely manner. If you have been reading up on short stories as I advised, you will by now have become aware that one story might cover three weeks, or longer within its three or four thousand words, while another – *Leave Cancelled* by Nicholas Monsarrat, is a good example – could deal only with a few hours. Obviously the pace of each story must differ to compensate for the time span.

In a story covering a shorter space of time, the little details and events that happen will be far more meaningful, and make much more of an impression on the characters. They will feel emotions more intensely and brood about them, perhaps linking them with other events in the past. In a superficial, plotty story, the characters will go on from one physical happening to the next, and you cannot afford to let them stop and begin to dwell on each little detail.

When considering pace, we can also consider how and where suspense comes into a story. Suspense simply means that you never tell the readers everything until the proper moment has come to do so. There must always be something held in reserve, so that the readers have to keep guessing. At the beginning of the story, as we have seen, there is some sort of conflict or struggle apparent. It would be so easy to give the whole thing away – and indeed, some inexperienced writers do this – by revealing the outcome in the first few paragraphs. If you do this you will kill your story. Never let the reader know what the end of the story is to be until he gets there, otherwise he will have no reason to read any further.

Suspense means that as you are always holding something back; the reader, with only half the tale told, cannot stop reading. And try to plan it so that you do not reveal huge chunks of detail or explanation at any one point, whilst at another you are telling the reader virtually nothing. The story must unwind itself steadily, in the manner of a trickle of water from a crack in the rock. It must neither dry up nor overflow.

The exercise of suspense means that it must proceed relatively consistently, with perhaps just a little more urgency here, a little more holding back there, which will make for interest and variety. There should never be any suggestion that the story is out of control and telling itself all in a rush, or otherwise going off out of the writer's hands as the rock splits or the water stops completely.

Many people never realise that a story has a pace. But if you examine any good short story, you will see just how the writer has progressed, whether he has written the story with a fast or a slow pace, and how he has handled the suspense element. What surprises has he kept back, revealing them one by one, until the final revelation at the end? When you know the tricks, the scam is easy to spot, but that does not mean the stories are any less good.

Because one goes behind the scenes in a theatre and sees

how the scenery works, how the make-up is applied, how the wardrobe mistress has dressed the ghost or the dragon or the devil, and all the other tricks of theatre, this does not mean the magic must be for ever lost, since now you know how it is all done. The same with ballet. If you watch dancers at work, see how they strain and sweat as they perform incredible technical feats and lifts, you will never look on it in quite the same way again, innocently imagining the ballerina is as light as a feather as her partner tosses her around. But you will appreciate all the more the artistry and dedication that has brought the dancers to their pitch of perfection.

In the same way, when you see how a story has been planned and plotted, put together so that the pace is right and the suspense is kept taut, leading the reader on to the ending, you will not just enjoy the story but will appreciate that the writer has done a good job and admire his methods.

Turning to mood, Ralph Waldo Emerson had this to say: 'It depends little on the object, much on the mood, in art.' The right mood can make the whole story, the wrong one can mar it irrevocably.

Contrast the following two openings of short stories; here is the first one:

> When the first fine days arrive, when the earth awakens and clothes itself in green, when the warm, scented air caresses your skin, fills your lungs and seems to reach your very heart, you feel a vague yearning for an unknown happiness, an urge to run about, to wander at random, to look for adventure and gulp down deep draughts of spring.

And here is the second:

> Nina was going to take credit for the death of the Beatle, John. I thought that was in very bad taste. She had her scrapbook laid out on my mahogany coffee table, newspaper clippings neatly arranged in chronological order, the bald statements of death recording all of her Feedings. Nina Drayton's smile was radiant, but

127

her pale-blue eyes showed no hint of warmth.

The first of these is from *In The Spring* by Guy de Maupassant; the second from *Carrion Comfort* by Dan Simmons. You can see that they are very different in mood. You would never, for instance, think the second one was going to be about springtime folly, nor that the first was about some sort of ghoulish vampire activity. You need to establish the mood of your story right at the beginning – you cannot change it, once established – and keep to it throughout.

Think of the effect you want to have upon your reader. Do you want your reader to read the story in a cheerful, optimistic frame of mind? Or perhaps you want him to feel a shiver down his spine as he reads on. Is the story to have a lighthearted mood, or a sombre tone? Do you want to have him laughing, enjoying life to the full with your characters, or pondering deeply and darkly on the tragedies of existence? Consider all this before you start, and remember that mood pervades every part of your story. It will also affect the way your characters view things (as we mentioned in the last chapter) and the way they feel.

You want to aim to sweep your reader along with you into the mood you have chosen. 'Good writing is supposed to evoke sensation in the reader,' said E.L. Doctorow, ' – not the fact that it is raining, but the feeling of being rained upon'. Your reader should feel the right mood draw him into it, so that he actually seems to have passed through a physical experience after he has read your story.

Atmosphere is almost a part of mood. New writers imagine there is some trick about dragging the right mood or right atmosphere into a story, but in fact, every writer starts completely cold so far as mood and atmosphere go. You will need to learn that the trick is not to somehow get hold of the right atmosphere or mood, or discover it, but to actually *create it* yourself, building it up from nothing. The reason for this is that mood and atmosphere do not exist until you yourself have created them and worked hard at building them into something tangible.

Consider the creepy atmosphere and ominous mood of a ruined old church or abbey. Surely, if you allow your characters to step within these crumbling walls, the mood and atmosphere will automatically be one of horror and the supernatural. It cannot help but be there automatically.

Yet think for a moment – if this was a lighter story, the fact that everybody is chilled might be for no more prosaic reason than that they have been on a twenty mile hike across the moors, they have wet feet and the rain is trickling down on their heads through the broken roof. This scenario would suggest a hilarious atmosphere of smoky camp fires, sizzling sausages and the finding of dry nooks and crannies out of the rain for their sleeping-bags, rather than the supernatural.

The atmosphere you want to create must be in your mind from the start, but do not try to push your readers straight into it at the deep end, or the effect will be the opposite of what you are aiming for. A horror story where the horrors start on page one will have your readers giggling and wondering whether it is meant to be funny; amusing stories will fall flat if you pile on the agony before you have allowed your readers to get beyond the first paragraph. Build up your atmosphere carefully, adding to it as you progress.

SUMMARY

1. Pace is the speed at which things, events, incidents, happen in a story. Some stories are slow-paced, others are quicker.

2. Stories with more plot than character are generally faster-paced than those where there is a lot of character detail.

3. Depending on the length of time the story covers, the pace has to be adjusted to compensate.

4. In a slow-paced story, details and emotions, moods and feelings will assume more importance than in a fast-paced story.

5. Suspense means keeping something in reserve, so that you

have never revealed the whole of your story until the right time has come to do so. The readers need to have something they do not yet know, or they will stop reading. Do not give away the end of your story within the first few paragraphs.

6. Do not reveal detail and explanation in large sections, while in others there is no real development of the story. This gives an unbalanced effect. Try to keep the flow of the narrative consistent and steady.

7. Mood is very important and you must establish the mood of your story right from the opening lines. When considering mood, think of the effect you want the story to have on your reader.

8. Remember that the mood of your story will affect the way your characters think and feel, as well as how they view things.

9. There is no such thing as the right atmosphere and mood to use when you start a story. It is up to you to build up your atmosphere and mood and keep them going. They do not exist until you create them yourself and build on them.

10. All atmosphere and mood, whether creepy, amusing or whatever, is relative and can spring from the same set of circumstances.

11. Start off slowly and do not overwhelm your reader with mood and atmosphere in the opening lines, or you will lose your effect.

15
WHERE TO END

From the *Daily Mirror*:

'*Movie mogul Sam Goldwyn complained to Dorothy Parker: "You and your wisecracks. I told you there's no money in wisecracks. People want a happy ending."*

'*She replied: "This will come as a shock, Mr Goldwyn, but in all of history, which has held billions of human beings, not a single one ever had a happy ending."*

In life, there are in fact no endings, happy or otherwise. Endings are highly artificial, and bear as little resemblance to reality as the rest of your story. They have to be worked for in order to round off your plot and bring your story to an aesthetically pleasing close.

We have already examined the place where the story must begin – where the moment of crisis is at hand and the struggle or conflict is about to commence. Where does the story stop? This question worries many new writers, but the answer is a simple one. The story ends when the moment of crisis has passed and the struggle or conflict is resolved. This is why is it so important to be aware of exactly what a short story consists of. Once you are aware that you begin with a struggle, conflict or problem, you will have no trouble in seeing when your struggle or whatever has been resolved, and in knowing that here is the proper place to end. There will be no question of plodding gamely on and on, waiting for some sort of sign that tells you the ending has arrived, just like that, out of nowhere.

This need not mean, however, that there is a definite and final cut off to your story. Most stories do not end in such a concrete sort of way, they are open-ended and often leave the reader to fill in the final details for himself.

Quite often, the story may appear to be still continuing, but what has probably happened is that the story itself has resolved its own struggle and then a new struggle or problem has arisen (which by rights belongs in a second story).

As we have seen when discussing characters and plot, incidents and action constantly arise from the interplay between the characters, and a final end if your characters are real ones, is a difficult thing to achieve, since such a thing would never happen to real people. However, once your own particular moment of crisis has been passed safely and your own particular struggle or conflict has worked itself out, that is where the end of your story must fall. Whatever happens afterwards belongs, by rights, in the reader's mind or in another story.

One thing which is often recommended is to write the end of your story first, as that way, you know where you are going. It might well work for you, but on the other hand, you may discover that once you have written yourself out in this sort of way, you will lose the impetus to write. You need to be very careful about writing yourself out or talking yourself out in any way whatsoever. Do not tell people what you are doing, and discuss ways and means in great detail or start writing endings which are emotionally fulfilling to you. You may lose the whole thing, since you will have no motivation once you have gone through the satisfaction of ending, to go back and start off with the beginning and the hard work in the middle.

Keep things to yourself, until you have written your first draft at least, and if you must tell somebody, then keep it to one helpful person whom you can use as a sounding board. Emotional give and take between yourself and other people will result in a lot of talking and very little writing getting done.

My own feeling is that it is a good idea to know what your end is to be, and to have a fairly clear idea of what you are aiming at, but to keep this very much in your mind until you get there. Not only might you talk or write yourself out, but you might find the ending changes as you proceed, and a much better one emerges from your subconscious. Never be afraid to alter your story as you progress. Even if you have a wonderful ending in your mind when you start to write, and you do not want to change it, and then something much less effective (you think) creeps in, this is because your story is a living creation, it is fluid and alive and is finding its own level, and its own end.

The ending of a story marks the climax in the resolution of your struggle or conflict. The worst thing you can do is to let it fizzle out like a damp squib. Tensions must mount, there must be something to indicate that this is the big moment, the final resolution of your tale. The readers must have several reactions to your ending. They must be satisfied that the conflict or struggle has been properly dealt with and that the problem in all its various aspects is now settled. Maybe it was not the ending they would have wished for, but if it was morally and artistically the right one, they will accept that it is right for this particular narrative.

They must feel too that it was a good ending insofar as it left them with a sense of finality, a feeling of completion. Half-endings or anti-climaxes spoil this particular effect, so avoid these at all costs.

Many people feel there has to be a twist at the end of every story. If you have been studying short stories you will by now have realised, of course, that this is not the case It is not always necessary for there to be a twist at the end, or even a surprise, and in some stories any attempt at a twist would spoil the whole thing.

Perhaps, towards the middle of the story, the reader might have begun to suspect what the end might be, and enjoyed the sense of inevitability as events did work themselves out so that what he suspected was correct. Twist stories again usually belong in the superficial categories where there is not a great deal of deep characterisation. They are more plotty than studies in character, though there can be surprises and twists even in a very complex story. The twist does have to be believable and acceptable, though, and should have the ground laid for it so that it is not so surprising that the readers think the wrong ending has been tagged on by mistake.

Lists have been made of the different types of endings a

writer can use. To quote F.A. Rockwell: 'You'll find that most modern stories have one of the following kinds of endings: Summation; Ideological; Antennae; Anti-Climax; Reversal; or Gimmick.'

These sound ominous, and if I was a new writer, I would be backing away from such technological talk. It is bad enough trying to put a story together without having to know whether you are heading for an Antennae or Reversal ending. Many new writers feel that the more technological jargon they are familiar with, the more writing terms they can trot out to friends and acquaintances, the better a writer they will be. But in fact, I can assure you that creating by numbers, so that you can give a label to every part of your story, will not help you to write well. Indeed, the technology might well hamper your natural creativity. You are not aware of it, but your brain and your subconscious would have been perfectly capable of coming up with a Reversal ending if that was what your story needed. And if that was the right one, you would have instinctively understood the Reversal process (where the situation at the beginning of the story is reversed at the end, that is all) without having to have it spelled out for you. It is worth remembering that people who talk about the various processes of writing may be very interesting, but it is the people who do the writing who are writers.

Do not make things difficult for yourself. Work through your struggle or problem to the climax, and give your story a good end and some appropriate closing lines when the right time comes.

Often, new writers are not sure where the end is, and continue to write on because they do not know how to stop. There is only one way to stop, and that is to write no more. But of course, there are good and bad methods of ending. So, as we did in the beginning, we are going to examine some reader-friendly endings of stories anonymously, with a list further on in the chapter. Here they are.

READER-FRIENDLY ENDINGS

1. He stepped into the shelter and came out carrying a spade

in one hand. He took the reins of the tall grey horse with the other hand and let it away.

Head low, staring at the ground before him, he led it past the corral, across the almost dry stream bed, and stopped at last by the straggling row of stunted cottonwoods.

He looked up. The other men had followed him.

'Don't be a fool,' one of the men said. 'Drag him out some-where and let the buzzards and coyotes have him. He wasn't no more'n an animal himself...'

'No,' the man in the buckskin shirt said. He looked back past the shelter, on into the vast empty distance where the trail of a tired horse led north-eastward towards the far lowering of the ridge and returned... 'He was a murderin' thievin' son-of-a-bitch. But he was a man.'

Quietly, bending to the hot task in the clean sun, the man in the buckskin shirt struck the spade into the red-brown earth.

2. 'I didn't mean it,' said the boy, starting for the door... 'He must've been crazy, laughin' like that. He thought I was somebody else, too. Kept callin' me Wallace.'

Lieutenant Pisano was silent. He stood looking into the open suitcase. Then he turned to the boy, his face thoughtful. 'Wallace...?' he said with growing comprehension...

3. 'It's like watching some deformed thing trying to move when she gets up. But don't dare to come near me. Don't dare to put those flabby hands on me. I'm not so decrepit that I'll accept your touch, crawling on my skin.

She knows. She waits. And suddenly, blindingly, I see the sadness in the eyes behind those awful spectacles.

I'll pay the waitress while you get your coat on James.

Oh, Lucy, Lucy! Where did we go wrong? Where did we lose each other? Oh, my Lucy, forgive me – forgive me – !

4. And now was acknowledged the presence of the Red Death. He had come like a thief in the night. And one by one dropped the revellers in the blood-bedewed halls of their revel, and died each in the despairing posture of his fall. And

the life of the ebony clock went out with that of the last of the gay. And the flames of the tripods expired. And Darkness and Decay and the Red Death held illimitable dominion over all.

5. And the people fell upon their knees in awe, and the nobles sheathed their swords and did homage, and the Bishop's face grew pale, and his hand trembled. 'A greater than I hath crowned thee,' he cried, and he knelt before him.

And the young King came down from the high altar, and passed home through the midst of the people. But no man dared to look upon his face, for it was like the face of an angel.

COMMENT

Amazingly enough, it is much more difficult to find a story with a good, taut, tight, artistically pleasing ending than it is to find reader-friendly opening lines. Obviously even the greatest writers have difficulty in thinking up wonderful endings, so if you have a little trouble with yours, you are in good company. But the one rule if you are getting desperate and feel you just cannot stop, is simply to take the pen away from the paper, or your fingers from the typewriter keys. A somewhat ragged finish is much more acceptable than a lot of unnecessary rambling and wandering round the point when the story is long since over.

The titles of the endings above are as follows:

1. *One Man's Honour* by Jack Schaefer.
2. *Robbery, Robbery!* by William Link and Richard Levinson.
3. *Tea for Two* by Tom Elliot.
4. *The Masque of the Red Death* by Edgar Allan Poe.
5. *The Young King* by Oscar Wilde.

One problem that worries new writers is – how long should my story be, so that I know where to stop? We have already seen that each story has its own ideal length, and you would be wise at first, while you are learning the art, to pay more attention to the shape of your story, where you begin and end with regard to your plot, as we have just discussed, than worrying about how many thousand words you can allow yourself. When you have grasped the rudiments of short story writing, you can then start to worry about length and suitability for markets and try fitting your idea into a certain length. Most markets allow a leeway either way, so you are never likely to be tied down to the very last word.

SUMMARY

1. In life there are no such things as endings. They are highly artificial, and have to be carefully created in order to round off your plot and bring the story to an aesthetically pleasing close.

2. A story ends when the crisis has passed and the conflict, struggle or problem has been resolved or overcome.

3. The end might well be open-ended, leaving the readers to fill in details. A stone-wall end rarely works well unless the story is extremely superficial.

4. Every story is concerned with its own special problem, struggle or conflict and working it through. Other conflicts belong in other stories, not this one. Each story keeps within its own limits.

5. You might prefer to write your ending first, so you know where you are heading, but be careful not to let your story and the emotive ending get talked out or written out or you will lose your motivation for starting at the beginning.

6. Do not be afraid to change your plot as you go along and use a different ending if it seems a good idea.

7. Readers do not want a damp squib at the end. They want to feel satisfied and that your ending is the right one for this

story, even if it is not what they had hoped for. They need to feel the story has been completed.

8. You need not feel obliged to include a twist ending, but if you do, the twist must be believable and acceptable to the reader.

9. Jargon will not help you to create a good ending and your own subconscious is perfectly capable of coming up with all the inspiration (and information) you need. Trust yourself and have confidence in your own mind.

10. The only way to stop is – to stop.

PART IV
A WRITER AT WORK

16
A WRITER AT WORK

One of the best ways to learn any skill is to watch an expert at work. With writing this is seldom, if ever, possible since writing is such a personal thing. It happens between the writer's brain, heart and hand (and typewriter or word-processor) and is done when alone.

As the next best thing, however, this section will consider the work done by myself on one of my short stories, published in a collection entitled *The Ebb Tide and Other Stories from Cornwall* by Weavers Press Publishing. First we will read the story, and then I will talk you through the writing of it, making comments on where the ideas came from, what happened as it was being written and any other points of interest. You should begin to get a fairly clear idea of how I set about writing a story, though it has to be pointed out that no two stories are the same and they do not develop in the same way. And of course, other writers will have their own methods of working, which might be different to mine.

So first, the story:

SHADOW PLAY

Sitting in the deep bay window that juts out over where the steps go down to the sea. High tide, it seems to lap at the very foundations of the house, each ebb and flow wearing away the solid rock so that I can see, almost in an eye-blink, that eternal patience crumbling the last fragment, the house collapsing, being swallowed up. Or only the echo of the house. It won't be there then.

Now, though, it is present, it is real. Window seat with padded chintz cushions supports me; glass is cold against my nose; velvet hangings are soft to my touch. I look at my hand, lifted to stroke the claret coloured draperies. My hand. This strange, bony appendage with blue veins and gawky knuckles. It doesn't look like my hand, but it is. I exist. I live. This is my hand, I tell myself.

I stare at it for a few moments, wondering, then let it drop, pick up the pen and notebook beside me and turn from the grey day outside, the fog heavy with fine droplets of water that cling to the window panes, the presence of the sea muted, invisible. Here there is warmth, the reassurance of thick red carpets, the spaciousness of the high ceiling, the cream walls with mirrors catching the light in prisms and throwing it back and forth, from side to side.

Today, the future starts.

I pause, consider the words I have written. It depends whether you have a positive or a negative attitude. Today is the watershed, the line between what has gone and what will come. Today the future starts, but today, equally certainly, the past ends. Unborn tomorrow, said Omar, and dead yesterday. And in between, the shifting seconds of now.

I rise, go across to one of the mirrors, stare at myself with impersonal curiosity. How boring to see the same face every time I look in a mirror. I twist my head to try and catch an angle of myself that I have never seen before, some small glimpse to relieve the dullness bred by familiarity. It doesn't work. It never works. Always the same me that looks back.

How old is my face? Time means nothing to the soul. Age is just a word. Every year of my life I have looked different, but to myself I am always the same. Trapped in the now of the present. Maybe even memory is an illusion. I think about Time. The ticking of my watch, the beat of my heart. On and on, for ever and ever. Yet each tick, each beat, is the only one that exists. The last has slipped into the past; the next may never happen. How slender is the thread. We live always in the moment of awareness. What is real may change by the time we draw another breath. Where was I, a heartbeat ago? Now I am here, but where was I then? I cling to the reality of my own pulse, afraid in sudden panic that it may stop. I feel the blood pounding in my head so that I can see nothing. Feel the dimensions sliding from my grasp. Run from the room in smothering terror, calling:

'Edwin. Edwin?'

Where the hell is he? Anger stabs through me. He should be here when I need him. He's here often enough when I don't, when I want to be left alone. Hovering, protecting, caring, until I could scream.

His voice floats up from the depths of the hall below the wide, shallow staircase.

'Is that you, pigeon?'

Emerging from the study doorway, bald head shining, shirtsleeves neatly confined by old fashioned gold cuff-links, brown spaniel's eyes watching me anxiously as I go down the stairs.

'Is something the matter?'

The reality of smooth wood under my hands has brought me back. The terror is gone, and the anger is taking on form. It's settled on Edwin's baldness, his stockiness, and especially the concern in his eyes. I feel such revulsion that I know I have to get away.

'I thought I'd go for a walk,' I say, through stiff lips.

'In this fog?' he says doubtfully, just as I knew he would. Irritation sharpens my voice. This is a familiar ritual.

'Why shouldn't I go for a walk?'

He sighs.

'I'm busy at the moment, but I'll come for a walk with you later.'

Is it worth the effort of arguing, asserting myself? This morning, I haven't got the strength. I say nothing.

'Why don't you go and do some writing?' he suggests, and mutely, heavy limbed, I turn and begin the climb to the top floor and the cliché Edwin's faithfully observed – the attic converted into a 'work-room' where I have spread out my papers and books, typewriter and pen. Stiff with resentment, I shut the door behind me, reject Edwin, reject the world. I don't want to write. I feel tired, exhausted. I sit on the big patchwork cushion on the floor, lean against the wall, curl myself up small, think about living and dying.

*

Man, said Rousseau, is born free, but is everywhere in

chains. Huddled on the cushion, I wonder about freedom, about chains. Was I born free? A free spirit with free will? Or was it all predestined, my path laid out for me? Were the chains already waiting even as I was laid in Maeve's arms for the first time? Could I have broken away, smashed the bonds that linked me in my small dependency to the two creatures who had fashioned my earthly body from their own?

Could I have piped infant defiance into Maeve's face or denied those other hands, that, in their male strength, protected his child from scavengers? Should I have somehow realised the enormity of his crime, recognised the dark wings beating round my head when, a scavenger himself, he swooped from the clouds to violate, even as the tears streamed down his face, the flesh of his own living lamb?

The weakness was in him, not in me, yet it was round the mind of his child that the chains grew tighter, the trap closed. Should I have, with atavistic wisdom beyond my years, passed judgement on him, pronounced sentence, cut through my chains with an epigram and left him kneeling, shamed yet still assured of his soul's salvation if he confessed in humility the frailties of his flesh?

'Mea culpa', he weeps, through his fingers, his gaze turned inward to the dark, secret, ecstatic sin. And Maeve beside him, her hair a cloud, the nails of a martyr's cross bleeding from her unseeing eyes where they have pierced the soul and life is dripping away.

'Mea culpa'. Maeve forms the words with her lips.

For them the richness of the ruby lamp, gold stars, penitence thick as incense on the air, abasement, chastisement, absolution. But the unspoken reality grows in the womb of their child like a monstrous cancer, until the time comes when it breaks forth into hideous form, splitting the shell that has carried the burden for so long.

Red slashes across my wrists released that devouring spectre of guilt into my own image, my shadow, my shape, my doppel-ganger. It was a confrontation sealed with blood. 'I am you and you are me. You can never escape me. I will never leave you.' I can see her clearly, myself, my other self, her white skin charred, festering. She is laughing across from the mirror, even as I hide my eyes. I can hear her laughter beating from the four walls, beating me down, battering me to the floor.

'Let me die. Oh, God, let me die.'

But instead I feel those familiar hands that fathered both her and me, a travesty of tenderness. I hear Maeve's scream splintering the air into a million shattered pieces. God is Love. Love is his hands, his lips, his voice, and Maeve's prostrate body weeping tears that will never end for my soul. Love is the stain of my guilt, the image in the mirror that haunts me as I run from room to room, the sin that laughs down the corridors of memory like a scratched old record on the turntable of Time, playing itself in my head until I beat myself again and again at the floor so that my pain may silence it.

God is Love. God is Infinite. God is everywhere. There is no escape. But later comes the cleansing, the purging of my spirit. The realisation that I can leap the bounds of reality, forsake the substance for the shadow. I can see through the mirror. I see Lucifer strong and magnificent, the throne of God beneath him shrivelling. I see that black is white, that dark is light, that day is night. I am Judas, giving the kiss of love to my betrayer. I know myself, I am the image behind the glass, I am the alter ego cast by the sun, that runs on the ground and crawls with the worms. Nothing can confine me. I have found my freedom.

*

Chained then, but I am free as air. I am travelling from nowhere into nothing. I have no roots to pull me down. I never speak of the house in London, I do not want to remember it. And I have denied Maeve's memories of Ireland, wiped out the sound of her voice as, a third in our dark trinity, she mourned that I had tempted him, that I made him fall. I have rejected the prayers that insinuated themselves into my dreams, the earnest pleading for my salvation.

Maeve blamed herself because that was in her nature, and she blamed me because I was the reincarnation of that self, but not wispy and insubstantial, something formed from the mists and glimmers on lake water, dimmed through hours on her knees, weeping. I was the Maeve she might have been once, hair softly curling round white shoulders, eyes with their sooty lashes so deeply blue that they smote your heart. Not a wraith, but a vivid and vital being of fire, an enchantress. She never blamed him. It was her fault, and it was mine because I was her daughter and in spite of my unawareness, my innocence, the pattern played itself through a second time, and once again he was too weak to resist.

So I have no country. I am a wanderer. I can go where I please and do what I will. There is no Time for me. I regulate it myself, create my own days and nights.

Here, though, in this house, Edwin's reality rules me, as it did in the house in Hampstead where he and Mrs Edwards and the ghost of his mother had established their rituals long before he married me. Edwin and Mrs Edwards and the ghost of his mother cling manically to the chains of their lives. Familiar. Comfortable. A place for everything, and everything in its place. An evening for cleaning the silver, which must never vary. After I broke a cup from the Doulton tea-service, I was not allowed to wash up again.

'You don't need to, pigeon. Mrs Edwards would rather do it, as she has always done. You don't need to do anything.'

'But Edwin, I'd like to think I was being useful.'

His smile, indulging a child.

'You're a writer, you don't have to be useful. And after all, you're not strong yet, you've got to get well. I'll see to everything. Just don't worry your head about anything except your poems.'

Smothering, feeling the weight of yet another love grinding me down, stifling me, I accepted the burden and nodded. How hard is resignation when one's protest is not against evil but good; not against injustice but benevolence; not against starvation but a surfeit of sweetness.

In spite of his love for me, his devotion, even my physical presence is an intrusion. His mother's ghost still presides over the household. The mahogany-and-stuffed-velvet chairs that stand round the table in the dining room looking out over the sea, stood just so in the Hampstead house. The mirrors on the walls are filled with her image, her secretive smile. Mrs Edwards unfailingly washes, cleans, tidies as though a phantom finger will be run across surfaces looking for dust, a phantom frown pucker that imperious brow if there is a single deviation from the ritual established in the hollow, claret-draped rooms of the Hampstead house when, a red-cheeked wench from the country, Clara Dew as she was then, she tearfully attempted to accept her new life 'in service'.

After a while, her longing for green fields and apple blossom quivering in the spring sunlight, laughter in crystal droplets like spilled water from the pump, faded. Maybe there was a renewal of life when she managed to become Clara Edwards; maybe she hoped that the colours would come back into her world of coal scuttles and blacking and morning teas served behind heavy drawn curtains, the egg boiled for exactly two-and-a-half minutes, or else the spoon would be laid down without comment, but there would be no escaping the accusation in those eyes.

Maybe, but the face that smiles from the frame in her room, cap tilted jauntily as though to defy Air Force Regulations, was blown to pieces over the Channel. Sometimes Mrs Edwards plays Vera Lynn singing 'We'll Meet Again' and 'The White Cliffs of Dover' on her old cabinet gramophone, and enjoys an evening of tearful nostalgia. But using the right serving spoons with the vegetable dishes brings more balm to Mrs Edwards' soul than anticipating reunion with the laughing-eyed and shattered face within the frame.

A sea-gull has alighted noisily outside the little gable window, on the sill, taking me by surprise. Even as I gasp at the sudden violation of my peace, it struts, crying, and I exist in the now, the room taking substance round me.

I laugh, scramble to my feet, go across to pull faces at the gull. Beyond the window, the fog swirls. I am aware of the sound of the sea. Images flash through my brain. Red velvet turns to silver and palest green; upholstered chairs become unicorns tossing their manes like smoke upon the air – .

And then the sound of the Tyrolean cow bell that hangs in the hall echoes through the house. Mrs Edwards is telling us that lunch is ready. I am ravenous. I run down the stairs while the bell still vibrates. I am alive and life is suddenly very good.

*

Edwin is sitting at the round table in the dining room. Dishes on the snowy cloth sizzle invitingly. The glasses and knives catch the grey light. The room is full of small rainbows, and I feel so bursting with power that I could catch them in my hands. Edwin holds out my chair, seats himself opposite to me. We smile at each other, while we pile chops and vegetables onto the gold rimmed plates.

'Well, have you finished your work?' Teasing him.

'Yes, pigeon, all done.' His soft brown eyes rest on me with love. I look away hastily, beginning to eat.

'Did you write anything?' he asks.

'No, but I saw a sea-gull. It landed on the windowsill. It was a good idea to come here, wasn't it? Better than London. More elemental; you can feel the world turning.'

Edwin chews his food thoughtfully, a slight frown between his brows. I try to repair the breach.

'I mean, you haven't cut yourself off completely. Just semi-retired. And the rest of the time you can relax. Not feel so pressured.'

'No.'

I want to tell him about the rainbows within reach of my hands, the consciousness in this now, this moment, of El Dorado somewhere beyond the boom of the sea as the tide swirls below us, the glittering apples of the Hesperides lost in the mist outside the window. I can feel the longing to speak like a lump in my throat. I have difficulty in swallowing. I try to say something that will reach him.

'Shall we go for a walk after lunch, then?'

'If you would like to.'

It is impossible. But I try again.

'I'm thinking of the flowers hidden under all this fog. The crocuses are coming out now, you know, they always remind me of jewels, so bright. The pink shrub's got loads of blossoms – I think it's an azalea – but they're white aren't they? –

148

or it might be a camellia – oh, the romance of Marguerite Gautier – how lovely if we've got our own camellia – .'

Edwin grimaces suddenly.

'I'll have to tell Mrs Edwards to mash the potatoes in future, they're repeating on me.'

I shut my eyes momentarily. When I open them, I look for the rainbows knowing they will be gone. El Dorado is an echo of old fables, dead men's tales from beyond the Pillars of Hercules. The Hesperides, shores of the Isles of the Blessed, were never there at all. The fog weeps outside the window.

I eat the food and taste nothing. My hands move stiffly, like those of an automaton. Edwin talks about share prices. I nod, a half-smile fixed to my mouth. The silver scrapes on the gold-rimmed plates.

'Edwin,' I say desperately. 'What day is it?'

'Wednesday, pigeon.'

I'll hold onto Wednesday. And when we go for our walk, I know his hand will be there, his fingers gentle, possessive of mine. I'll have the stone flags of the path solid beneath my feet. The lilac bush by the gate will be dripping moisture. There's a road outside and the gulls will be calling.

I will ask Mrs Edwards for some bread. Give it to the gulls.

* * *

THE TALKTHROUGH

So how did this story come to be written? Well, in the first place, it started off as a novel. Yes, anyone can make the mistake of thinking they are writing a novel when in fact they are writing a story, as we have seen. The important thing is to find out which one you are really doing, which is right – and then to do it.

The irritant which drove me here was a series of glimpses, flashes of the sort that appear in the story, of this heroine's strange and desperate state of mind, and the vivid traumas of her memories. I have to admit I did not consciously think in terms of theme, character, plot and so on, and I had no particular market in mind when I sat down to write. This was something I felt I had to externalise because it was haunting me so deeply.

In fact, there is a theme – there are several themes. The main one, perhaps, concerns communication – that however close we are to each other, however we love each other, we are separate entities and cannot know each other closely. This theme is rather sad – but there is a compensating and more uplifting one, which is that love will overcome everything, even the damage inflicted by false loves and the inability to communicate with each other.

The plot, as such, concerns the heroine who was subjected to incest by her father (and, unwillingly, by her mother) and blamed by them so that she took on herself such a burden of guilt and sense of sin that she felt unable to live with herself and attempted suicide. At some point, she was rescued by an older man, Edwin, who loves her deeply and whose care and protection she resents, but at the same time, clings to and is grateful for, though whether she loves Edwin is somewhat ambiguous.

This ambiguity reflects and pervades the whole story. Her feelings towards her parents, her feelings towards her 'work', her feelings towards the house where she lives, to the 'housekeeper', to her husband, all reflect a pattern of dependency and need, rebellion, withdrawal, renewed dependency and need. Whether she will ever break this pattern, we are not sure, but in the plot proper, the moment of crisis gives us a hint that there might be a change – or, on the other hand, she might have permanently accepted her position and given up the struggle. The story is really open-ended and leaves a lot for the reader to decide.

The actual plot proper takes place within a few hours of a morning, when the heroine stops to consider her position and to come to some sort of conclusion about it. Only her mood and her attitude changes, but she finishes on a note of small initiative – even in her own home, she feels she must ask Mrs Edwards for bread, but she herself will give it to the birds. Whether this is the start of a process of learning to assert herself, or a gesture that acknowledges her acceptance of her submissive role, is for the reader to decide.

This plot arrived in my mind from chaos, and I have to admit I wrote the story largely by instinct. When I started the original novel, I included other characters, particularly a psychiatrist with whom the heroine was conducting a deep relationship. Eventually, I realised that their involved discussions about death, suicide and so on, were not only unutterably depressing but were pure self-indulgence on my part, since the subject interested me. I had written three chapters – about 60 pages – when I suddenly saw the light and thought: 'It's a *short story*. Of course!' All the work I had done on my proposed novel had in fact been preparatory work for the story, so I scrapped the novel and went back, picking the bones of my story out from the mass of extraneous material. I lifted chunks of text, discarded others, and pieced the story together, linking the whole thing into a story form. The rest I threw away.

Now for a few technical details. You will notice that I did not give my heroine a name. I felt she was too close to the reader, too close to herself, too deeply vulnerable and speaking from her soul, for her to be pinned down with a name. The effect would have been quite spoiled if Edwin had come out of the study and yelled up the stairs: 'Are you all right, Sonja?' Or however lovely the name might have been. The reader is in her intimate confidence, and knows her beyond her name, as it were.

Her mother is named, but here I had to make a change when I was editing the text. The name I originally gave her mother was Erin, which to me was the one that was right. But it was pointed out to me that the names of Edwin, Erin and even Mrs Edwards were all similar and might be confusing. I altered Erin, though that is still the one which sums up the character for me.

Her father, the villain of the piece, not only has no name, but she refuses to mention him in any other way than by calling him 'he', which expresses her loathing of him and of the whole relationship to which she was subjected.

Many varied bits and pieces of material went into the melting pot. For instance, although the story is set in Cornwall, the house and stretch of coast that was in my mind when I was writing was actually situated in, of all places, Llandudno in North Wales. And the atmospheric description of a church, summing up the way in which the heroine's parents confessed their sin and found peace which was denied to her, drifted into my mind from recollections of a visit to a beautiful church in Ostend while on holiday years ago.

You will notice that I have described Edwin briefly, but only as he would appear to the heroine, who, as with most people in a close relationship, no longer notices features such as colour of eyes and hair. The fact that she chooses one or two particular features to brood on and feel resentful about is typical of this sort of close living together, when one person can become driven to distraction by a simple habit or characteristic in the other.

She herself is not described in any way. If you can read the minds of your characters clearly, especially your central character, so that they become alive to you, you will find you can bring them to life for the reader without description of outward features. We do not know what colour eyes and hair this woman has, whether she is young or just seeming young and immature because of her mental condition. But hopefully she comes across as an interesting personality and one we can identify with because of the thoughts she shares with us.

A good deal of what she feels, we are told, but there is a lot – about her relationship with Edwin, for instance – which is left for the reader to work out himself.

I have used a style which is not strictly correct grammatically. Sometimes the sentences contain no subjects – the first and last, for instance. This serves several purposes. It makes us feel close to the heroine as though we are looking over her shoulder perhaps, as she jots down notes in a diary; and it also helps to put across her mental turmoil and gives us a picture of someone who is not stable emotionally and is unable to express herself coherently at times. But if you want to juggle with the rules of grammar and write things ungrammatically, remember that one of the things to remember about writing is that you learn the rules first – including those of grammar – before you start to break them.

And, as we have seen, you only break rules for a reason, and you have to be aware of what that reason is.

Defining this story on the Story Content scale, it comes pretty low down, since there is very little 'plotty' plot and the story concerns relationships and emotions. Compensating for the lack of plot, there is a great deal of concentration on the characters and their feelings. Background is added, including the background of Mrs Edwards, so that we get a detailed picture of the setting in which the heroine finds herself. The reader should feel, at the end of this story, that he has been through an experience with people he has come to know very well.

The viewpoint here is of course that of the heroine, who writes in the first person. She is able to tell us her deepest feelings and the fact that sometimes she is reluctant to speak directly about what happened to her, and refers obliquely to her father and her own traumatic recollections of the past, helps us to understand her hang-ups about her past and the conflicts in her present. We should, however, feel if this story has been successful, that if asked, she could bring a great deal more evidence to light, and answer questions about the smallest details. We must feel that we know Edwin and Mrs Edwards through the heroine's comments about them and attitude to them. They do not have a chance to put themselves across, we have to build up our picture of them through her eyes and through the attitude she takes towards them.

There is little dialogue, but this underlines the fact that the story is about difficulties in communication. What dialogue there is takes place mainly in the scene at the end, where the heroine makes an effort to break the barrier – and fails yet again. Sometimes you may feel – as I did in this story – that you have gone for too long without using any dialogue, and that you really should give the characters something to say. But if the dialogue seems wrong, or whatever you put in seems awkward and strained, trust your own judgement and do not force it. There is no obligation to have your characters hold long conversations with each other. In the end, here, I used only the minimum of dialogue until the little scene at the end when the heroine tries to break out of her little cell of silence.

The pace of the story is comparatively slow and the mood intense. The heroine is trapped in a sort of time warp from which she cannot escape, like a fly in amber. The story is serious, the atmosphere tragic rather than inclining towards any sort of lighter atmosphere, and we have already seen how the ending – open-ended as it is so that it might be hopeful or it might be subdued – comes about.

PART V
THE COMMERCIAL PRODUCT

17
HOW TO EDIT AND PRESENT YOUR MANUSCRIPT

So you have finished the first draft of your story. What next?

Many new writers are blissfully unaware that there is a next. They visualise editors eagerly queuing to publish their masterpiece, with no further effort required on their behalf except to make sure there are enough copies to satisfy everybody concerned.

But in fact, the first draft of your story could (and probably will) well be only that – a first draft – with several other drafts to be worked on. Do not take it for granted that once you have reached the end, that is it, there is no more work left to do. It is possible, if you are that sort of writer, that you have been working on your manuscript as you go, and that your first draft is practically complete.

More likely than not, though, if you are inexperienced – and this includes people who have written a lot but never had any success with what they wrote – you need to look over your manuscript with a critical editor's eye and pull it into shape.

In general, editing and polishing can only be done after the story is written. Once it is completed, you can view it as a whole, as an entity, not as something that is still developing and therefore still changing its form and shape. When completed, it stands before you, you can view it in its entirety, and you should doff your writer's hat and put on the hat marked editor. Any story will benefit from a good going-over by an editor if the editor is sympathetic and constructive. You will be both of these where your own story is concerned, of course, but do not be too easy on yourself when you come to edit the pages you have written. Acknowledge the faults you might have made, put the errors right, do not try to argue about why they should be left in. All that we are concerned with is showing off your story in the best possible light.

You might wonder why I am telling you to go over your story with the eye of an editor. You, after all, are a writer – is it not up to the editor to whom you submit your work to do the editing? This is a misconception which has probably put paid to the careers of a good many writers. The theory that you send off your work in its first draft, and the editor has a look at it and says: 'Ah yes, with a bit of editing, this could be a masterpiece' just does not hold water.

An editor does not want to see your half-finished first drafts, or even a second, slightly more coherent version. He wants to see the finished product, editorially polished so that there is hardly a single correction or alteration to be made when he sends it to be printed. He will recognise this sort of thing as the work of a professional. Manuscripts which need cutting and scoring and pulling into shape – even if they might be potential masterpieces – will only reinforce his conviction that he is dealing with an amateur who has no idea of the ropes. And no editor (except for some we shall meet later) has time or inclination to start nursemaiding amateurs through a very competitive and cut-throat business. You will stand no chance at all of being taken seriously.

How to Edit

You may feel at a great disadvantage, since it has never occurred to you that you could actually do the work of an editor. What is involved, you ask. How do you go about editing your story? Here is a simple guide to the sort of things an editor does, which you can easily do if you try, and which can benefit your work immeasurably.

1. Try to detach yourself emotionally from the story before you. It is simply a story someone has written, which you have

to edit. Do not allow yourself to remain so deeply involved with it that your feelings cloud your judgement.

2. Read through the manuscript and cut out – yes, cut out – any unnecessary words or phrases. You will find they positively scream at you. Particularly, look out for adjectives, adverbs and descriptive phrases which you do not need.

3. Read through the manuscript again and cut out phrases or sentences which duplicate each other or are repetitive. Cut out ramblings around the point and clarify any points that are vague and woolly.

4. If possible, get the whole thing retyped now and read it once more. Is the storyline clear? Are there any points left which seem vague? Are the characters well drawn? If there is any uncertainty over clarity of plot, definition of character, then revise or rewrite the relevant sections so that the story runs smoothly and there are no awkward bits. This goes beyond the scope of what an editor would normally do, but certainly a sub-editor would see the weaknesses and would know how to put them right. You have to be your own panel of editors and sub-editors.

5. Consider your opening sentence. Whatever you finally decided to start off with, is this a good, gripping opening? If not, try to start with a better one.

6. Is your ending crisp and clear, something definite, not just a weak fade? If it is not very good, try to strengthen it.

7. Is there any part of the story where you are aware that some work needs to be done, but you keep telling yourself that 'nobody will notice'? If so, rest assured that this section will stand out like a sore thumb – and get to work at once. The fact that this is probably a particularly awkward section only means the need for clarity and precision is all the greater, so you should devote all the time and attention that is needed for repairs or rewriting.

8. What about your title? Is it good, apt, suited to the story? If you cannot think of anything brilliant, do not worry. Greater writers than yourself have made do with boring titles –Tolstoy, for instance, with *Master and Man, Father Sergius* and *Hadji Murat*; Chekhov with *The Party, An Unpleasant Business* and *A Nervous Breakdown*. Often, an editor who likes your story and wants to publish it may ask your permission to change the title, and a fresh brain may come up with a new slant on the whole thing.

It is worth mentioning here that an editor who wanted to publish your story might also ask your permission to cut or sub it in some way. Your first reaction might be hysterical fury, and a sworn declaration that he will alter a word at his peril! But pause for a moment. Often, it is good editing that makes a story, particularly if the writer is new and inexperienced. Try to detach yourself from your work and consider his suggestions without feeling emotionally betrayed. You will probably find that these cuts give the story a tighter, taughter feel and liven up the whole thing.

It is rarely, and should be never, that an editor cuts or edits a story without asking your permission. He will not be behaving in an accepted manner if he does so, though I have known it happen. In such a case, all I can suggest is – try to get some sort of compensation for this type of bad treatment, and avoid doing business with that particular editor in the future. Whereas it is accepted that an editor may cut an article or sub it, fiction is usually treated with a little more deference. But if the editor should ask your permission to cut, remember that he is an expert who has been in the business for longer than you have, and think very carefully before you flatly refuse. Negotiate, if you need to, and make your own suggestions for cuts, but bear in mind that he probably thinks the story will benefit from the cutting – and that should be the aim of everyone concerned.

PRESENTATION

Once you have finished your writing and other work, and have your final copy of your story – the best you can possibly do with it – you will need to consider how best to present it if you are going to submit it to an editor, agent or other interested party.

The simplest way is the best – typed or printed on a word-processor in double spacing, with margins both sides of at least 1" and good margins top and bottom, using one side of the page only. There is no need at all for fancy details – editors are interested in the story, not in whether your WP can justify the whole thing, or whether you have a particularly decorative script with curlicues all over the place. Some people take the attitude that the more the story looks as though it is 'in print', the more favourably the editor will look upon it.

In fact, the opposite is the case. Editors are annoyed by finicky detail in presentation and consider that people who submit beautifully laid out, carefully planned, almost-'printed' stories have just got to be rank amateurs of the rawest sort. So aim to be clear and readable, that is more than good enough.

What else should you enclose with your typed copy? A brief letter to the editor mentioning the name of the story you are submitting for his consideration; a cover page for the story bearing title, name of author (your name or your pseudonym if you have one) and your own name, address and telephone number. You could usefully include on this page the length (number of words) of the story. On your final typed copy itself, number the pages consecutively; attach a clean cover sheet at the back, and using the right size to cope with the bulkiness of the manuscript, hold together with a paper-clip. On no account use pins to keep your manuscript together – editors loathe them, and they give the game away right from the start.

When you send off your manuscript, enclose a stamped addressed envelope of the right size in case of return.* One further point needs to be made. You should never, ever, let your last copy of your story out of your sight. Always keep a

*When sending manuscripts abroad do not send stamps. Enquire at your Post Office for International Reply Coupons.

duplicate, even if it is scribbled over and generally messed about. Never send your last copy or disk out of your possession, as if anything should happen to it – which has been known – you would be in the unfortunate position of having to rewrite the whole thing. And that is not a pleasant prospect. Besides which, it is amateurish and silly. So always keep a copy.

18
MARKETS FOR YOUR WORK

Since we first examined the commercial approach to writing a story we have, hopefully, progressed a great deal and become reasonably proficient at the short story form as an art. We have served an apprenticeship, and perhaps now we can consider tackling a story for a particular market. The rules for market study are the same as they were at the beginning of this book, and here we shall consider the various types of market open to the short story writer today.

Reference works to guide you as you consider the various publications and publishers are *The Writers' & Artists' Yearbook* (A & C Black) and *The Writer's Handbook* (Macmillan) which are published annually and are continually updated. The scene in America is covered by the Writer's Digest Books publication *Writer's Market*. Do not forget that there are many opportunities abroad to sell your short stories.

It is often assumed – increasingly as would-be writers become more sophisticated – that the most sensible action to take as a first step to success is to acquire the services of an agent. But while it is certainly true that an agent will be aware of openings which are not made public to the ordinary writer – of publishers who are planning an anthology of ghost stories, for example – there are very few agents who will be interested in unknown, untried writers who approach them with a handful of short stories.

Agents want to feel their investments will pay off handsomely, and they are unlikely to show interest in anyone who writes short stories unless that person has a distinguished track record, has written book-length manuscripts as well, or in general displays a remarkable talent they cannot ignore.

So you may approach agents, but do not be discouraged if

they are not very helpful. Remember that the odds are against you here right from the start. You are far more likely to start building up a cuttings file of your own work through your own, perhaps more modest, efforts.

LENGTH

It is when we consider submitting work to publishers that the question of length comes into its own. If you are writing for your own pleasure, or can allow yourself to run to whatever length you like, then you hardly need to consider how long a story is going to be. But in a magazine or periodical, an editor needs to know exactly how much space a story will take up, and because he can work this out from the number of printed words which he knows will fill up a certain space, he will ask contributors for stories of that length. Too few words will leave him with a gap – too many will over-run the allotted space. This is why editors stipulate the length of stories they require, not because they have a whim to include only stories of 2,000 words, say, in their publication. The reason why length matters is thus practical and professional, and editors are not likely to accept stories which are longer, or shorter, than the length they have requested.

The knack of writing to a certain length, which you may find difficult at first, is one which will come with practise. Often, if you over-write, you will find that cutting and editing will not only benefit your story in the ways we have discussed, but will bring you down to the correct wordage. It is far better to over-run than to make your story too short, for while it is always possible to cut, it is practically an impossibility to make fiction longer except by padding it with unnecessary detail or incident, unless you re-write the whole thing.

Some new writers are under the impression that in order to find the length of a story, you need to count every word. This would be asking too much of a writer, and there is a way of calculating the length of anything you write. First of all, take an average over perhaps ten pages written or typed in the way you would normally set out a page, of the number of lines per page. Then take an average over about twenty lines from different parts of the manuscript, of the number of words per line. Multiply the number of words per line by the number of lines per page, and that will give you the word count per page. It will also enable you to calculate, by multiplying the number of words per page by the right number of pages, the total word count. No editor will reasonably expect you to count up every word you have written, nor to worry about short lines of dialogue or half-lines at the end of paragraphs. So long as your estimates are reasonably accurate, that will do.

1. AND OTHER STORIES

Many new writers of short stories never even consider writing for magazines or periodicals, but see their work right from the start as a collection, a volume of short stories, bound in book form. If this is your aim, I am afraid that here again, you and others like you are in for a shock. Though publishers will go to great lengths to assure you that their only criterion when accepting manuscripts is quality, it remains a daunting fact that few books by new writers make the grade, and a collection of short stories by an unknown author has even less of a chance than a novel.

Publishers do admit that they are more inclined to consider work submitted by agents than unsolicited manuscripts from people they have never heard of, but as we have seen, there is a Catch-22 situation where agents are concerned. Unless you are utterly determined to follow your dream and aim for a volume of short stories as your contribution to literature, you would be wisest to spread your net as widely as possible and try to get a story published anywhere so that at least you are on your way and have something to show for your efforts.

We have to face the fact that the prospect of getting your stories published in book form is pretty hopeless – or extremely remote, to say the least. The best we can say is that genuine talent, genuine quality, is so rare that it is hailed on all sides when it does appear. If your work is genuinely good enough, if it has the magic spark and is worthy of publication, then sooner or later, it will find a publisher. But otherwise, be prepared for a long, hard haul with nothing but a lot of frustration at the end of it.

2. THE WOMEN'S MAGAZINES

Times have changed since the days when the covers on bookstalls included general magazines that ate up fiction such as *Argosy* and *John Bull*. Now, it is the magazines aimed at women which offer the greatest scope for the short story writer, and their requirements range from extremely stereotyped stories of the 'True Confessions' type to elegant and sophisticated quality fiction in the glossies.

If you aim to write for this market, follow the rules for market study – even male writers will find crime slots and twist ending short fiction here alongside the romance. And what is more, new writers are often given active encouragement if they show promise. At the headquarters of D.C. Thomson & Co. in Dundee where *My Weekly*, *People's Friend* and *Annabel* are produced, you can obtain Guidelines on writing for these magazines, and editors will work with you if they think you have potential.

Meantime, to help you along, here is what the Editor of *My Weekly* has identified as the sort of story she is looking for: 'There is no single aspect that's all-important in writing a good short story. For *My Weekly* it's more a case of combination of the right ingredients. In other words, a strong, unusual theme coupled with credible characterisation, backed up with believable development and a hopeful, uplifting outcome.'

Nearly all the women's magazines are looking for romances, and if you can produce stories of this sort, you might well start doing a brisk trade. You will find as you study the examples in your market research that romances differ from the more general sort of story we have been concerning ourselves with, in that they have rules which you have to follow. Even if you think the best and most plausible ending artistically is one which leaves the heroine desolate and mourning her lost love, you have to grit your teeth and end with, if not true love and wedding bells, at least an embrace and the prospect of an engagement.

Here is a list of useful rules to help you write romances:

1. The story is generally told from the point of view of the heroine, rarely that of the hero, and only occasionally by an outside observer.

2. The heroine is generally aged about twenty, and the hero some ten years or so older, compensatingly if her age should rise. You can sometimes have stories where the heroine is a widow (rarely a divorcee) perhaps with young children – often this situation involves the children bringing the hero and heroine together in some way.

3. Animals are very popular and can also be a way of bringing hero and heroine together. They also make a good excuse for conversation between characters, and take their owners out to walk them or look for them.

4. Most romances are family-orientated and have a settled family life somewhere in the background, even if (as often happens with romantic heroines) they are orphans. Devoted elderly aunts who phone regularly and prove to have an unexpected streak of worldly wisdom are popular, as also are younger brothers or sisters who cause chaos.

5. Heroines may have other boyfriends or even potential husbands, but it is generally understood that they do not sleep around. Although some sex has been allowed in romance in recent years, it is safest for magazine stories to make it clear that your heroine is probably a virgin.

6. Heroes have to be a good prospect both socially and financially. Heroes never fail exams (they never take exams) or get sacked from their jobs, unless this is simply to reveal their genius in other directions. You should not have a heroine falling for a drifter, a drop-out, a man with nothing. Heroes are never losers: even if they are doddering round a castle in Scotland which is falling to pieces about their ears, they will be a

Laird, even if a penniless one. They always come out on top.

7. It is accepted that hero and heroine feel some strong feeling for each other as soon as they meet. This may seem to be dislike, even hate, and can express itself in verbal battles, slanging matches and an apparent antipathy that turns, as events progress, to respect and love.

8. They have to overcome some sort of obstacle to their love, which can be in the form of previous boy/girl friends, family disapproval, misunderstandings about their feelings for each other, the contributions of their children (the hero might be a widower with children who are probably heading for their early teens) or even the hero's dog conducting a running battle with the heroine's cat.

9. A romance must have, if not a happy, at least a hopeful or uplifting ending.

If you study the different women's magazines, you will see that some of them cater for the traditional romantic story where the woman remains unfulfilled until she has found her man; others like career-girl heroines who approach love on a basis of equality. Sometimes the lovers may be older folk who meet at a night of Old Tyme Dancing, or they may be a teenaged Romeo and Juliet.

It cannot be emphasised enough that in order to succeed in this or any market, you need to study that market, not just flip through a few magazines and then write something you think the readers ought to want to read. And the other great rule when writing romance is that you must believe completely and utterly (while you are writing, at any rate) in what you are doing.

Romance is not something that can be dashed off with your tongue in your cheek. You need to be able to identify with the values you are upholding and to write with complete sincerity. Humour is not barred – often humour can add spice to a love story – but any form of cynicism will damn your story from the opening lines.

Contrary to what many people believe, romance is neither some sort of trashy poor relation to great literature, nor is it easier to write. Good, well written romantic stories are just as much of a credit to their authors as the most literary undertakings. And what is more, the demand for romance remains constant, while the demand for literary works is often comparatively small.

3. THE RADIO STORY

Many writers of short stories do not consider one of the best outlets there is for their work, and the place where they might have more chance of meeting with success than in print –on the radio. Excitingly, the radio story can give you a great deal of scope, in that it can cover areas other than those required for love stories and romance; but you do have to be aware that radio has its own limitations.

Bear in mind when writing for radio that your story will not be read by the eye, it will be read by an actor or actress who will interpret it to the listener. And so, as with plays for the stage the listener, like the audience, cannot stop and turn back to refresh his mind on some detail or remind himself who such-and-such a character is. And taking the matter even further than the stage, the listener to radio cannot see the action and so can easily become confused.

If you would like to try and write for radio, make sure you listen to as many radio stories as possible and familiarise yourself with the do's and don'ts of radio technique. Radio stories should ideally be written especially for this medium, and a story which you originally wrote to be read by the eye will in all probability not be suitable.

In a radio story, you have to attract the interest of the reader immediately, since if he hears nothing that arouses his attention in the opening minute or so, he will switch off. So your story must plunge into the action, the crisis, the problem, conflict or whatever, within the first few lines.

The first character who appears will be the one with whom he will identify, so radio stories are often told in the first person, where the 'I' who is doing the narrating is the central character. You have to be careful, too, not to introduce too many characters too closely together, as this will cause the reader confusion – remember he is listening blind – and in fact, large numbers of characters are not a good idea in a radio story at all. This is why many of them concern relationships or some sort of action between just two or three people – or even more personally revolving around the central character alone.

It is advisable too, to avoid crowd scenes where large numbers of people get involved in the action. Not only will the listener be too confused to identify the characters as they speak, but the reader of the story will find it difficult to create so many different voices.

Since the writer for radio needs to keep his cast of characters down to a few, it is quite likely that the story will be intense rather than superficial, and involve detailed problems of personality and characterisation rather than be a fast-moving thriller full of action. People writing for their local radio might well discover that the local dialect, if there is one, and local traditions and customs are welcomed as a background for stories. Local radio stations try to keep up the individuality and personality of the area they cover, and expert knowledge of the locality often goes down well.

The storyline itself must be kept simple because, as we have already seen, there is no turning back the page or going back to the beginning to find out who somebody is. The listener cannot stop the story to check on anything, and it is the writer's job to make sure that the need to do so never arises. Keep things simple and easy to follow, so that the listener does not find himself confused, for once his attention has been allowed to wander, it is highly unlikely that the storyteller will manage to get it back.

There are certain subjects which you should avoid when writing for radio. Anything that will shock, offend or otherwise upset unsuspecting listeners will never be accepted no matter how well written the story is. Remember that, unlike a reader who can inspect a magazine or book before she buys it or borrows it from the library, a listener has no warning of what is about to come. It is the duty of those who select stories to be broadcast to censor what does get on the air, and, bearing in mind that many listeners to the radio live alone, and might be frail, elderly or otherwise vulnerable, it is highly unlikely that tales of brutal muggings or forced entry and rape, or unsettling details of any sort, will be welcome. Something with a bit of humour in it, or a lift to the spirits, can be just as representative of life today as sordid details of violence and crime.

If you think you would like to write for the radio, there are two options open to you. You can contact the BBC (all addresses can be found in the writers' handbooks mentioned previously) and ask for details of any openings they have for stories. For a long time, stories used to be broadcast regularly in the *Morning Story* slot, but this moved to the afternoon, and might well have moved again by the time this book has passed through the pre-publication process. The BBC will provide you with information on their requirements as to length, style, subject matter, and anything else they feel deserves mention. They have been noted in the past for dealing within a week or so with any stories submitted to them, so you should not be kept waiting months for an answer.

The address and phone number of your local radio station (your second option) will be in your local telephone directory, and if you approach them with a query as to who would be the producer or presenter to speak to about submitting your stories, you will generally find you will be helpfully received. If you have been listening regularly, you should in any case be aware by now of which particular slots feature stories, the length and type they seem to prefer, and the person who deals with that particular programme.

Do not neglect your local commercial radio stations, either. Though they mostly do not use fiction, there is always the possibility you could persuade them to make an exception. Maybe they have just never been asked!

One point to bear in mind is that the radio story has to fill up a certain number of minutes rather than a certain number of pages. In order to calculate whether your story will run for the right length of time, take an average of about five pages, as you would normally set them out and read them aloud as though you were reading them on the radio yourself (you might indeed be asked to, especially on local radio). Time your reading, and take an average so you know roughly how long one of your pages will run to. Then you can calculate lengths and times.

Reading your work aloud is also a good tip to help you hear what the listeners will hear when your story is read out on the radio. You should be able to learn from what you hear so that stiff dialogue or stilted description can be loosened up to sound more natural. Remember always that there is an immense difference between what the eye reads and what the ear takes in – learn to recognise this difference and act accordingly.

4. IN GENERAL

For writers who want more freedom in what they write, more of a chance to spread their wings – and also those who may still be a little unsure of themselves as yet – there is a world of which the general public is largely unaware, but which could help you get your break into print.

Listed in the writers' handbooks are the names and addresses of many of what are generally known as Small Presses. There are many others, which you will be able to discover when you begin to investigate this market. They are small – sometimes one-man or desk-top –publishers, or even groups, co-operatives or societies which print their own little magazines, and these often take poetry and short stories and practically anything the editor likes the look of. Further details of these can be found in the magazine *Writers News*, which carries up to date information on many obscure markets which are not commonly known.

Small Presses run their little magazines on a shoestring usually, and generally sell only on subscription, but they will send sample copies if you want to study them. Many are subsidised by bodies such as the Arts Council, and it is in these modest publications that you could find your work getting thrillingly into print.

There are also various elite literary magazines you might approach, which again take poetry and literary prose works, but if you want to aim this high, remember that you need to study the market. The *London Magazine*, for instance, is hopeful in encouraging new writers to submit their work so long as they have studied what sort of work the magazine takes. They claim they do accept work by new writers, though they only accept about one in fifty stories by unknowns submitted to them. Never mind about the 49 who didn't make it, though – you could well be the one who did! But always study your market first or you will still be in with the 49 failures at the end of your career.

As well as Small Presses and lesser known little magazines, there is another world which is ramshackle and far-flung and, like the main part of an iceberg, is hardly ever visible to the public in general. This the world of competitions. Here you might not only get into print or see your story form part of a collection in a book, but you could win relatively big money.

Lists of competitions can again be found in those invaluable writers' handbooks as well as in *Writers News*, and if you keep your eyes open when visiting your local library, for instance, you might see a competition by your local Arts Council or some other body being advertised. There are many chances to win in competitions – some of the women's magazines run them as do festivals up and down the country – so long as you follow the rules and remember that there will be many other people submitting mediocre stories and even (as we mentioned at the beginning of this book) stories which are not really stories at all.

Wherever you submit your work, remember that it is your ambassador, representing you to the public. Never think shoddy work will do, or that one of the Small Press magazines, for instance, is glad of anything so you need not take any trouble. Keep right from the start to the highest standards, and always do your best. You are a professional – behave professionally. And sooner or later, if you have what it takes, you will get your break and you'll be on your way.

19
PAYMENT
AND RIGHTS

There is no set payment for short stories. You might expect to be offered several hundreds of pounds from one of the glossies, while some of the Small Press magazines pay only in free copies of the issue in which your story appears. You will be offered a fee, and whether you accept it or not and sell your story to that particular market is up to you.

Never, except under exceptional circumstances, sell your work outright, copyright and all. Normally, any magazine that offers to publish your story will expect to buy what we call the First British Serial Rights* (in this country). Some writers feel it necessary to mark the title page of their story with the words: 'First British Serial Rights offered' and to affirm their ownership of the copyright with the copyright mark © followed by their name. In fact, there is no real need to affirm that you hold the copyright, as in this country it is automatically yours as soon as you write a story, and there is no need to register it in any way. But anxious minds are set at rest if the writers feel they have made the position clear.

When you are considering a market, look in the small print usually on the inside page, where the editorial details are situated. It generally says what rights the magazine likes to buy. If it does not, and you are offered a fee for publication, ask what rights the magazine wishes to buy for that fee. Most publications are not concerned with anything except the First British Serial Rights, though occasionally you might be asked for All Rights, which will include the rights to publish in other countries or in books, anthologies and so on.

There is no need to become paranoid about your work, as it is highly unlikely that any magazine has some ulterior

---

*This simply means the right to publish the work for the first time in the territory stated, and has nothing to do with publishing the story in the form of a serial.

motive and is trying to prise your work from you. Most usually follow their standard practice, whatever that may be. And bear in mind that it is not very likely that you will be able to sell a story two or three times more (Second British Serial Rights and Third British Serial Rights) once it has been published, though sometimes this can happen. It is wise, however, to think very hard about parting with copyright, as this means you will be giving up all claim to your story.

Occasionally, a magazine may not consult you with an offer of publication: it might just go ahead and publish, and the first you know about it is when your complimentary copy and cheque arrive. I have known people to feel distressed because they were not informed that small changes had been made, and to feel the fee was not enough. Unfortunately, these hiccoughs can happen, but remember that whenever you send an unsolicited manuscript to an editor, you are in effect indicating your willingness to abide by his decisions, and since all editors are busy men, you cannot expect an in-depth correspondence about your story if he suddenly has a gap to fill, and seizes on your manuscript to fill it.

Think professional and remember that publishing is a rat race, you are lucky if you get your scam over successfully and get yourself into print. One day the tables will be turned, and editors will be asking *you* to consider writing something for them.

PART VI
A STORYTELLER'S LIFE

20
A STORYTELLER'S LIFE

WHAT SUCCESSFUL WRITERS SAY

Writers have different views on almost every aspect of writing, but we can learn something from them all. In their various ways, they embody the views of both genius and professional hack, but each person who contributes to the great body of literature in whatever capacity plays a valuable part. We may hope that we are not just hacks; we can be sure that we are probably not geniuses!

While Mickey Spillane claimed that: 'A writer is someone who always sells. An author is one who writes a book that makes a big splash,' Boris Pasternak described the writer as 'the Faust of modern society, the only surviving individualist in a mass age. To his orthodox contemporaries he seems a semi-madman.'

As for what the writer does, Erskine Caldwell points out: 'I think you must remember that a writer is a simple-minded person to begin with and go on that basis. He's not a great mind, he's not a great thinker, he's not a great philosopher, he's a storyteller.' Malcolm Cowley adds that the writer 'is a person who talks to himself, or better who talks in himself.'

And according to Anais Nin: 'The role of the writer is not to say what we can all say, but what we are unable to say.'

How to recognise whether you are a born writer? These rare birds can easily be identified according to Delmore Schwartz, who informs us that: 'Writers are self-indulgent, full of self-pity, forever seeking reassurance, constantly occupied with what they consider the proper conditions of work, and the next thing to invalids in their demands upon life.' H.L. Mencken adds: 'My belief is that all authors are essentially lonely men. Every one of them has to do his work in a room alone, and he inevitably gets very tired of himself.'

This far from flattering – though often accurate – picture is further coloured by the comment of John Hall Wheelock that 'Most authors are in a state of gloom a good deal of the time...'

If you want to be a short story writer – and a good short story writer – this is the sort of lifestyle you can expect. It is not easy to be a writer, and if it were possible to have a choice in the matter, most writers would prefer to be contented, well balanced people who were able to take life placidly as it came without having to agonise over the inventions of their mind. Unfortunately (or perhaps fortunately, who can tell?) most writers have been writers since they were born, whether they have actually written or not, and they do not know what it is like to be 'ordinary'. It has indeed even been pointed out that writers who fail have to suffer not only the agonies of being a creative spirit and all that entails, but the double blow of failure and rejection as well.

Many people do not realise that being writer is a full-time job, and takes more out of the writer than if he had spent the day labouring at some physical task. Emerson points out that: 'The writer, like the priest, must be exempted from secular labour. His work needs a frolic health; he must be at the top of his condition.' Writers, too, often have their faults and failings. They suffer from the jealousies that spring from lack of confidence, and can be ruthless if their career is threatened or their place about to be usurped.

Lilian Hellman observed that: 'Writers are interesting people, but often mean and petty' while Sherwood Anderson noted that most writers 'are awful sticks to talk with'. Malcolm Cowley made the cryptic observation that: 'Authors are sometimes like tomcats: they distrust all the other toms, but they are kind to kittens.'

Agonising apart, however, many writers have expressed their delight in their chosen career or vocation. Flaubert said sweepingly: 'Writing is a dog's life, but the only life worth living.' While Raymond Carver enthused: 'Writing's not terrible, it's wonderful. I keep my own hours, do what I please. When I want to travel, I can. But mainly I'm doing what I most wanted to do all my life. I'm not into the agonies of creation.'

Tom Clancy echoes this: 'Writing is so much damned fun. I play God. I feel like a kid at Christmas. I make people do what I want, and I change things as I go along.' If you do not have something in you of this same delight in what you are doing, there is probably something wrong somewhere. Even if it does not stay with you all the time, you should get enjoyment from your writing. If it seems like hard labour every step of the way, then you are probably wasting your own time and that of everyone else. Mind you there are times –many of them – when you will probably feel like giving up on the whole idea. It happens to the best of us, and as Peter De Vries remarks: 'I love being a writer. What I can't stand is the paperwork.' Do not allow yourself to get despondent when these moments of doubt occur. You have to learn to find the strength within yourself to go on. Writing is, as we have noted already, one of the loneliest jobs in the world.

Much valuable information can be gleaned from what successful writers have said about their work and about writing in general. Here is perhaps one of the most useful of all, a quotation from John Barth: 'You shouldn't pay very much attention to anything writers say. They don't know why they do what they do. They're like good tennis players or good painters, who are just full of nonsense, pompous and embarrassing, or merely mistaken, when they open their mouths.'

This is very true. Many people sift through quotes from famous authors, and read interview after interview with successful writers in the hope that the success will somehow rub off on them, that they will somehow unearth a secret that will ensure them instant fame and instant success. But there is no such secret. As John Barth so rightly says, most authors have no real idea of how they produce their work. It is indeed often a case that 'those who can do, and those who can't, teach'. Most genuine authors are far too busy struggling with their own writing to spare the time to teach others; while people who like to instruct those who know less than themselves find this prospect much more agreeable than venturing with their talent into the melting-pot and perhaps finding that, in the long run, they do not measure up.

However, we can take it that the comments of successful writers are those of experience and a knowledge of writing which only comes from actually writing – and writing well. The fact that they contradict each other does not matter. Every writer works differently. But somewhere among the comments uttered by those who have proved their worth in the field of writing, there will be something that will strike a chord within you, get your mind working and your imagination racing.

What do writers aim for? What lies at the end of the road? Success? Fame? Fortune? Fame has been variously defined as 'a feeling. Like what you get after a pill' by Joyce Cary; by Jules Renard as 'a constant effort'; as 'proof that people are gullible' by Emerson; while Tobi Sanders says simply: 'I want it.'

Writers in general seem rather bewildered when confronted by fame. Whatever you have in mind when you start out on your career, rest assured that what you will find at the end of your climb up the ladder of success will be something entirely different to what you thought would be there.

Fame is such an odd thing. As H.L. Mencken says: 'A writer is always admired most, not by those who have read him, but by those who have merely heard about him.' Andre Gide makes the penetrating comment that: 'Enduring fame is promised only to those writers who can offer to successive generations a substance constantly renewed; for every generation arrives upon the scene with its own particular hunger.'

'Odd things happen to book writers when they become famous,' says Ronald Sukenick, while Martin Amis believes that: 'Early acclaim won't harm a writer if he has the strength, or the cynicism, not to believe in that acclaim'. 'Fill an author with a titanic fame and you do not make him titanic, you often merely burst him,' says Frank Moore Colby.

But while most new writers would take their chances with fame, the ultimate aim of everyone should be to write well, to produce good work. Here, great writers often speak of their own inner doubts and fears.

Samuel Beckett has declared that: 'Suffering is the main condition of the artistic experience', and Isaac Bashevis Singer explains how: 'Every creator painfully experiences the chasm between his inner vision and its ultimate expression. The chasm is never completely bridged. We all have the conviction, perhaps illusory, that we have much more to say than appears on the paper.'

Kingsley Amis reveals that: 'I find writing very nervous work. I'm always in a dither when starting a novel – that's the worst time. It's like going to the dentist, because you do make a kind of appointment with yourself.' And Susan Sontag tells us: 'I am profoundly uncertain about how to write. I know what I love or what I like, because it's a direct, passionate response. But when I write I'm very uncertain whether it's good enough. That is, of course, the writer's agony.'

In the constant struggle to write well, it is generally accepted that writers, along with other artists, spend a great deal of time in a state of almost constant anxiety. Georges Simenon declared that: 'Writing is not a profession but a vocation of unhappiness. I don't think an artist can ever be happy.' However, George Santayana interestingly observes: 'If artists and poets are unhappy, it is after all because happiness does not interest them.'

We have a large body of opinion that writing is 'pretty crummy on the nerves' (Paul Theroux), 'a nauseous process' (Rebecca West); 'hell' (William Styron); 'so difficult that I often feel that writers, having had their hell on earth, will escape all punishment hereafter' (Jessamyn West). What are the rewards for the terrible striving, the constant agony that most writers experience?

These come when the writer has the sense that he has created something good, stretched himself to the limit, gone far beyond the mediocre and the superficial. The joy and satisfaction which a writer experiences when he can feel he has done a good job can only be understood by another writer who has had the same experience.

'Good writing excites me, and makes life worth living,'

said Harold Pinter, while Charles Baudelaire wrote rather more racily: 'On the day the young writer corrects his first proof sheet he is as proud as a schoolboy who has just gotten his first dose of the pox'. James M. Barrie confessed that: 'For several days after my first book was published I carried it about in my pocket, and took surreptitious peeps at it to make sure the ink had not faded.'

Some writers even feel they are setting up some sort of monument for themselves, since if their work is good enough, it will live on when they are dead. George Ade commented wryly: 'Posterity – what you write for after being turned down by publishers', while Jorge Luis Borges added: 'When writers die they become books, which is, after all, not too bad an incarnation.'

All authors live in hope, and Hilaire Belloc perhaps summed up the secret dream of every storyteller in this couplet:

'When I am dead, I hope it may be said:

'His sins were scarlet, but his books were read.'

READING GUIDE

Having been advised to start reading short stories, you may have little idea where to begin except for obvious places like women's magazines. So here are a few hints to help you on your way.

One of the most important qualities a really good story will possess is that it will haunt you for the rest of your life – and I mean that literally. For instance, when I was very young, perhaps twelve or so, I read a horror story in an anthology on the bookshelf at home. It has stayed with me ever since, even though it was not until quite recently that I discovered the name of the author, which I had not, at such a young age, bothered to note. No wonder the story had gripped me so much: it was work of Guy de Maupassant, whom we have already met, one of the consummate masters of the short story.

This particular story was called *The Horla*. Read it for yourself and see whether you too fall beneath its spell. De Maupassant's short stories are available in collected form, and you can usefully study his work for its sheer storytelling quality, its vitality and sense of living. Also note that the writing seems utterly effortless.

The second author I want to mention is Daphne du Maurier, whose short stories have been published in many selected editions. She too possesses this haunting quality, and once again I can remember reading some of her work in my early teens, finding that it clung to my mind for years afterwards. Study her stories for their characterisation, their masterly detail, their depth of involvement, their use of suspense and tension, their beginnings and endings.

We have already tasted the stories of two brilliant storytellers whose works will give you tremendous insight into differing writing styles and the use of atmosphere and mood.

185

I bring them once again to your attention, as many people do not realise that Edgar Allan Poe and Oscar Wilde both wrote short stories, as well as poetry and plays. Study their stories carefully, especially noting their mastery of scene-setting and description.

Damon Runyon and Ernest Hemingway, both American, developed their own very individual styles of writing and their short stories will illustrate for you how the world into which the reader is drawn can seem so much more vivid than the world outside. Notice that Runyon seems to let his stories flow along garrulously in his own particular Broadway jargon that has been described as 'Runyonese', while Hemingway appears to give only the barest minimum of information to his readers. Both to wonderful effect.

Other classic writers whose stories should be readily available to you in libraries are Saki (the pseudonym of Hector Hugo Munro); O. Henry (real name William Sydney) and Somerset Maugham. Saki was a writer of wit who kept his stories short but used the space to the best possible effect; O. Henry was master of the twist ending (remember we have already mentioned his story *The Gift of the Magi* used to illustrate how shape and form can enhance your work); and Somerset Maugham's stories often deal with conflict between different social classes, and in particular with the ways in which white people in the tropics were affected by their environment. But even though there are less British rubber planters leaving for the tropics with their delicate, neurotic wives nowadays than when Maugham was writing, the studies in relationship that you will find in his work can be examined as wonderful examples of the writer's art, as well as his excellent craftsmanship.

Read the work of Ray Bradbury, one of the greatest sci-fi storytellers, for his economy and for his ability to transport the reader into unfamiliar situations with consummate skill.

Read Katherine Mansfield for her brilliance in exploring the minds and emotions of children and women.

Most of these authors can be easily found in libraries or sometimes bookshops if you would like to have your own copies to study, but naturally, they represent only the tip of the iceberg. I have used them as examples because I myself found them enjoyable to read and was inspired by them – hopefully to the benefit of my own writing career.

If you want to read more up to date authors as well as classic masters, a query at your local library will soon point you in the right direction. And make sure you read on every level, including stories you might think poor or trashy. Learn from your own analyses of what went wrong, why they are poor, as well as learning to appreciate why those which are classics still retain their quality. Find your own personal favourites, the ones which will stay in your mind for the rest of your life. Perhaps at some time in the future, your own stories might be recommended as classic examples to new generations of writing students. Aim for that sort of quality – and good luck.